The Terai Community and National Integration in Nepal

Hari Bansh Jha
M.A., Ph.D. (Economics)

ADROIT
Adroit Publishers
New Delhi

ISBN : 978-81-87393-44-3

First Edition : 1993
Second Edition : 2017

Published by
ADROIT PUBLISHERS
4675/21, Ganpati Bhawan, Ansari Road,
Daryaganj, New Delhi-110 002
Phone : 011-23266030

Distributors
AKHIL BOOK DISTRIBUTORS
email: akhilbooks@yahoo.com
akhilbks@gmail.com

Typesetting - Gaurav Graphics, New Delhi, INDIA
Printed at: Milan Graphics, New Delhi, INDIA

CONTENTS

Preface

Of Nepal's three geographic regions, the flat land of Terai which is also called Madhesh lies in the southern part of the country bordering Indian states of Bihar, Bengal and Uttar Pradesh. The Madhesh region forms only 23 percent of Nepal's total geographical area; but it inhabits over 51 percent of country's total population of 28 million. Because of presence of more than half of the country's total population in the Terai, Nepal's identity has changed from a country of hilly people to the country of the plain people. The original inhabitants of Terai, who include caste-based Hindus, Muslims, Tharus and other tribal groups, are called Madheshis.

Until 1952-54, the Madheshis and Tharus formed 96 percent of the total population of Terai, but now their share in population in the region has declined partly due the migration of population from north to south and partly due to the exclusionary policy of the state. As per the government statistics, the share of the Madheshis is no more than a third of the country's total population.

But the Madheshis view the government figure to be grossly under-enumerated. As per the Washington, D.C. based Freedom House 2015 publication on "*Freedom in the World 2014: The Annual Survey of Political Rights and Civil Liberties,*" the population of the Madheshis is up to 50 percent of the country's total population.

Since 1950s, the state encouraged the migration of population from the hills to the Terai by introducing Malaria eradication programme in the Terai region. In this process, substantial sections of the Tharu population were evacuated from their land on one or the other pretexts. Those who could not tolerate the atrocities at home were forced to cross over the Nepal-India border and migrate to India. But those Tharus who did not leave their place were virtually made paupers as they lost their agricultural land at the hands of the hill migrants. The male Tharus had no option but to work as 'Kamaiyas" (paupers). Similarly, the female Tharus were forced to work as 'Kamleri' i.e. as labourers at the household chores of the newly settled hill migrants. Thus, the landlords of the region were turned into labourers; while the outsiders became the virtual landlords in Terai.

Over the years, an attempt was made by the state to divide the Tharus and Madheshis, the two dominant ethnic communities of Terai, fearing their potential power. More than the Madheshis, the Tharus were projected as nationalists. But once the Tharus started making claim over their resources and their rightful place in the new constitution promulgated on September 20, 2015, they were equally targeted by the state.

Until today there is a gross misinformation about the Madheshis, who happen to be the only indigenous people in the country. Their civilization is as old as that of people living in any other part of the world. Mention of Mithila, which forms part of Madhesh, is found in Ramayanic period some 10,000 years back. But certain people treat the Madheshis as if they are of Indian origin who migrated to Nepal from India at certain period of time. In certain quarters, they are also labelled as Indians and often derogatory language is used by calling them 'Dhotis' 'Biharis' or 'Uttar Pradeshis' as if they came from Bihar or Uttar Pradesh province of India.

In Nepal, the Madheshis maintain a distinct culture different from the hill people. Unlike the hill people, they speak the same languages spoken across the border in India such as Maithili, Bhojpuri, Awadhi and Hindi. Most of these people have marriage relationship across the border in India. This is perhaps one of the major reasons why they have better affinity with the people across the border in India rather with their own countrymen in the hills in the same way as the Indian border inhabitants are closer to the Madheshi people in Nepal than people living in other parts of the country. This is so partly due to the open border between Nepal and India and partly due to the fact that there was no distinct border demarcation between the Terai region of present day Nepal and India until the Sugauli Treaty of 1816 some 200 years ago.

Until a few years ago, the international community had very little information about the Madheshi people of Nepal. Information on Madhesh and its people first of all flooded during the Madhesh uprising of 2007 in which 54 people were killed and hundreds others were injured. The government tried its best to cool down the movement through the use of force, but it failed. It was only after the government signed an agreement with Madhesh People's Rights Forum, Nepal on 30th August 2007 and ensured proportional representation of the Madheshis and other marginalized groups in state mechanism that the agitation was called off.

One of the major achievements of the first Madhesh movement in the Terai was that it raised people's aspirations. As a result, the Madheshi political parties formed United Democratic Madheshi Forum and launched stir in Terai again in 2008. Uprising in Madhesh subsided when Prime Minister Girija Prasad Koirala singed an agreement with the leaders of Madheshi Forum on 28 February 2008 for the formation of a federal state "One Madhesh, One State" with right to self-determination in Terai.

In the subsequent years, the ruling hill elites did little to meet their commitment made with the Madheshi leaders. After the deadly earthquake in Nepal on April 25, 2015, the leaders of four major political parties signed 16-point agreement to make constitution on a fast track basis. But due to the trust deficit, the Madheshis and Tharus who formed substantial chunk of Nepal's population were not included in constitution making process. Finally, the constitution was made against the letter and spirit of Interim Constitution 2007 and Supreme Court Verdict.

In the seven-provincial model of the federal constitution most of the Madheshi region was mixed with the hill states. Except the Province No. 2 that includes only eight out of 20 districts of the Terai all other districts were made part of the hill states. As if this was not enough, the electoral constituencies for the 165-member House of Representatives and 59-member National Assembly were fixed more on the geographical rather than population basis. Such an arrangement would compel the Madheshis to get further marginalized and remain in minority.

Also, the constitution diluted the arrangement of proportional representation system that was ensured in Interim Constitution 2007. Besides, the constitution denied the children of those Nepalese from reaching high positions in government organs who married with the foreigners. For this, provision was made to give such children naturalized citizenship and not citizenship by descent. Since the Madheshis marry mostly across the border in India, they were targeted by the constitution to avoid such cross-border marriages.

Because of serious flaws in the constitution, the Madheshis and other Janajati groups have been opposing constitution even before its promulgation on September 20, 2015. When the state ruthlessly tried to suppress the movement, the agitating Madheshi and Tharu groups had no option left but to impose blockade on the Nepal-India border for five months until the first week of February. In this Madhesh-centric movement 58 people were killed and thousands of agitators were injured.

In another development, the Madheshi diaspora in different countries of the world, including in India, USA,

Britain and Australia also opposed government of Nepal for its high-handed measure in suppressing the movement. Even the Madheshi issue was discussed in world forums like the UN bodies in Geneva and New York. Issue of inclusion of Madheshis and other marginalized groups figured prominently in India-Britain Joint Communiqué in 2015 and India-EU Joint Communiqué in 2016. The government of India and the USA appealed to the Nepal government to address the issues of the dissatisfied agitating groups in the constitution with a view to maintaining long-term peace in the country.

In the meantime, the government unilaterally amended the constitution, but that did not meet the aspirations of the agitating groups. Lack of sensitivity of the government towards the Madheshi issues compelled the Madheshis to join hands with the hill-Janajati (indigeneous) groups in their bid to oppose the constitution. A natural alliance was made between the two communities because the hill-Janajatis have also been discriminated by the state. And, a new twist was given to the movement when the agitating groups shifted the venue of the movement from Terai to Kathmandu.

Before launching Kathmandu-centric protest programmes from May 14, 2016, the Federal Alliance of 29 Madheshi and hill Janajati groups presented 27-point demands before the government, which included provisions like ensuring proportional representation in state mechanism and rewriting constitution. As the government was least sensitive towards the demands of the Alliance, the agitating groups picketed Singha Durbar, the government administrative wing, in Kathmandu along with the Prime Minister official residence at Baluwatar and organized rallies in various parts of Kathmandu Valley and also in Birgunj and Pokhara. Presently, they have been opposing constitution by conducting relay hunger strike.

At a time the Madheshi movement was at its peak, Mr. Akhil Sharma of Delhi-based Adroit Publishers approached me and asked if I could write a book on Madhesh. I took this as an opportunity to bring the second edition of my book on "The Terai Community and National Integration in Nepal" that was published in Kathmandu in 1993 by the Centre for Economic and Technical Studies in cooperation with Friedrich-Ebert-Stiftung of Germany. This was the first authentic book on Madhesh and Madheshis in Nepal that had come with facts and figures based on field survey on different dimensions of Madhesh, including its history, population, economy, politics, language, migration, citizenship and hosts of other issues.

However, I avoided making any change in the basic structure of the book because I found it as relevant today as it was over two decades ago. The issues related to Madhesh and Madheshis are more or less the same. Before I conclude, let me extend thanks Mr. Akhil Sharma of Adroit Publishers for publishing the book in time.

Centre for Economic and
Technical Studies (CETS)
Kha 4/541, Dhobighat, Lalitpur
Kathmandu, Nepal

Hari Bansh Jha
(Executive Director)

Preface of the First Edition

The present book is the study of socio-economic conditions of the Terai community, inhabiting the southern part of Nepal, bordering with Bengal, Bihar and Uttar Pradesh states of India. The Terai community who are also called Madheshis constitute bulk of the Nepalese population and they have a distinct position in the socio-economic and political structure of the country.

The book has been organized into six chapters. Chapter 1 deals with introduction to the Terai Region of Nepal. In Chapter 2, the social structure of the Terai has been described. Chapter 3 addresses itself to the language issue. Chapter 4 is concerned with migration and its impact on the Terai. Chapter 5 throws light on the economy of the Terai. In Chapter 6, the issues related to the national integration have been analysed.

All the important socio-economic issues related to the Terai community have been covered in this book. It could, therefore, be expected that the government, planners and policy makers of Nepal would be aware of the genuine problems of this community and thereby help resolve them. This will ultimately strengthen the present democratic set-up as well as the process of national integration in Nepal.

In this context, I would like to express my deep sense of gratitude to Dr. Heinz Bongartz, Resident Representative, Friedrich-Ebert-Stiftung (FES). New Delhi, for his financial support to the Centre for Economic and Technical Studies (CETS) for carrying out the research, organizing a seminar and finally publishing the book on the Terai community.

The FES is a non-profit, private research and educational institution, committed to the concepts and basic values of social democracy. Its wide- ranging activities in the field of political education and assistance to partners in developing countries incorporate—among others—comprehensive projects in the areas of societal development, labour relations, business, science, and culture.

I am obliged to Prof. Krishna Chandra Mishra and Prof. Gopal Singh Nepali of Tribhuvan University for their guidance in carrying out the study.

Thanks are due to the enumerators—Mr. Anil Kumar Karna, Mr. Jeebachh Raya, Mr. Lakhan Pandit, Mr. Lalan Jha and Mr. Ram Prasad Sah, who took all the trouble to collect information through the questionnaires from the field.

I am indebted to Mr. Bhadrakali Mishra, Mr. Fateh Singh Tharu, Mr. Mahendra Kumar Mishra, Mr. Akhileshwar Prasad Singh, Dr. Dambar Narayan Yadav, Mr. Bhrigunath Thakur, Mr. Banshidhar Mishra, Mr. Yadu Bansh Jha and all those intellectuals who shared their ideas with me about the problems of the Madheshi community.

I am indebted to Prof. Tara Kant Jha who extended all possible cooperation to me in organizing the seminar on the theme of the study at Janakpur. Thanks are due to the commentators and discussants who expressed their valuable views in the seminar.

Thanks are due to the staff of Central Library, CNAS Library, Nepal Bharat Sanskritik Kendra Library, etc. who helped me in this enterprise by making the necessary literature accessible to me for this study.

I am grateful to Dr. Yogendra Prasad Yadava, Associate Professor of English of Tribhuvan University, for editing the manuscript of this book.

I would fail to do justice if I do not thank the respondents of the different Terai districts who supplied me with all the relevant information needed for this study.

Lastly, I expect my readers to help me correct the mistakes, if any, in this book.

Hari Bansh Jha
(Executive Director)

Centre for Economic and
Technical Studies (CETS)
Kha 4/541, Dhobighat, Lalitpur
Kathmandu, Nepal

LIST OF TABLES

ABBREVIATIONS

A.D.	After the Death of Christ
CBS	Central Bureau of Statistics
CDO	Chief District Officer
CPN	Communist Party of Nepal
DDC	District Development Committee
GDP	Gross Domestic Product
HH	Household
HMG/N	His Majesty's Government of Nepal
M.A.	Master of Art
MP	Member of Parliament
NC	Nepali Congress
CPN (UML)	Communist Party of Nepal (Unified Marxist-Leninist)
NEP	New Education Plan
NGO	Non-Governmental Organization
NMEO	Nepal Malaria Eradication Organization
No	Number
NPC	National Planning Commission
NEPC	National Education Planning Commission
NRC	Nepal Resettlement Company
NSP	Nepal Sadbhavana Party
P	Page
PP	Praja Parishad
RPP	Rastriya Prajatantra Party

RVDP	Rapti Valley Development Plan
TC	Terai Congress
TDC	Town Development Committee
UDP	United Democratic Party
U.N.	United Nations
USAID	United States Agency for International Development
VDC	Village Development Committee
VOL	Volume
WHO	World Health Organization

1

AN INTRODUCTION TO THE TERAI REGION OF NEPAL

Meaning of the Terai

The word Terai is relatively of recent origin and is used interchangeably for 'Madhesh', which is derived from the Sanskrit word 'Madhyadesh' meaning the mid-country between the foothills of the Himalayan mountain in the north and the Bindhya mountains in the south.[1] People living in this region have been called Madheshis or Madheshiyas. Manu, the law maker of the Hindu society, also mentioned the Madhyadesh.[2] Mention of Madhesh is also found in Buddhist literature, e.g. the Vinaya Pitak.[3]

In this book, however, the Terai or Madhesh has been referred to the plain strip of the land lying within the boundary of Nepal in the south and not the land in India. Likewise, the word Terain or Madheshi refers to not all the inhabitants of the Terai but to the native ones of this region.

The Land

The Terai region is a flat plain land in the southern part of Nepal and is the home of over half of the total population of the country. Because of the change in population composition, Nepal has virtually been transformed from a classic mountain country into a predominantly flat, sub-tropical, and urban land.[4]

Geographically, Nepal is divided into three distinct belts: the Terai (plains) in the south, the hills in the middle and the mountains in the north. The Terai is an extension of the Gangetic plains of India constituting 23 percent of the total land area of the country.

The narrow plain strip of land of the Terai belt starts from the foothills of the Siwalik or Churia range of the Himalayas and stretches out upto the plain region of the Indian provinces - Bengal, Bihar and Uttar Pradesh. It covers an area between the Mechi river in the east and the Mahakali river in the west. The average length and breadth of the Terai are approximately 500 miles and 20 miles, respectively.

The Terai is divided into two parts, viz. Inner Terai or 'Bhitri Madhesh' and Outer Terai or 'Bahiri Madhesh'. The inner Terai consists of flat land north of Siwalik or Churia range in Sindhuli, Makwanpur, and Dang districts. The outer Terai, on the other hand, consists of 20 districts, namely Jhapa, Morang, Sunsari, Saptari, Sirha, Dhanusha, Mahottari, Sarlahi, Rauthat, Bara, Parsa, Chitwan, Nawalparasi, Rupandehi, Kapilvastu, Banke, Bardia, Kailali, and Kanchanpur. The present study addresses itself to the outer Terai.

The altitude of the Terai goes upto 250 feet above the sea level. Its climate is hot and wet during the summer and cold during the winter. The Western Terai is also affected by the hot desert air called loo during the dry summer. In the Terai, the monsoon lasts between July and September and the average annual rainfall is recorded between 40 inches and 60 inches.[5]

History

In the ancient times, the Terai happened to be the centre of Hindu civilization, culture and learning. Many places in this region had a distinct role in the body-politic of 'Aryavarta', the home of the Aryans in North India.

The Terai comprises Janakpur, the capital city of the ancient state of Mithila. During the Ramayanic period, Siradhwaj Janak, the twenty-second king of the Nimi dynasty, reigned over this land. He was Goddess Sita's father and Lord Ram's father-in-law. During the Mahabharat War, Kshemurti was the King of Janakpur, who supported the Kauravas in their combat against the Pandavas. Janakpur, however, ceased to be a capital at a time "when the rule of the kings of Mithila was replaced by the unique oligarchical republics of the Vrijjias; the capital was thereafter shifted to Vaisali, one of the most famous cities of ancient India".[6]

Certain regions falling in Mid-Madhesh formed a part of the Vajjian Confederacy, which during Buddha's time was at the zenith of their glory. Kapilvastu, lying in the western region of the Terai, was a developed city state. It was ruled by Suddhodan, Lord Buddha's father.

Historical records also show that Morang (Biratnagar), Saptari, Mahottari, Rautahat and Simraungarh were important principalities during the medieval period.

In 1097 AD., Nanyadeva, the King of Mithila region in the Terai, captured the Kathmandu Valley[7] of Nepal from his capital at Simraungarh and dethroned the two princes, Jayadevamalla of Patan and Kathmandu, and Anandamalla of Bhadgaon. He died in 1147 AD. Harisimhadeva (1294 AD.) was the last great king of the Nanyadeva dynasty. He was a great patron of learning, social reformer and warrior. Mithila made all-round development during his reign. It was he who introduced "Panji-prabandha' and 'Kulinism' and, thus, initiated the system of genealogical records among the Brahman and Kayastha castes of people in Mithila. He also introduced the sub-caste system in the society, which exists in the Terai even today. But he met a major set-back during the later part of his life when he was attacked by Muslim conqueror Sultan Ghiyas-ud-din Tughlak in 1324. He fled from Mithila and entered the Kathmandu Valley and established his reign over Bhadgaon. This was the second invasion of the Kathmandu Valley, incidentally by the same dynasty.[8]

Harisimhadeva and his descendants exercised effective control over the entire Kathmandu Valley. But the two local rulers of Patan and Kathmandu were left undisturbed as they acceptcd their suzerainty. The reign of the Nanya dynasty in the Kathmandu Valley survived for about a century.

In Kathmandu, there is a noted temple of Goddess Tulja Bhawani at Hanuman Dhoka Palace in the heart of Kathmandu city. Historians assert that it was Harisimhadeva who brought the idol of Tulja Bhawani from Mithila after his conquest of the Kathmandu Valley. This idol was originally brought to Mithila from Karnataka by Nanyadeva. In this connection, Upendra Thakur writes,"...a particular point of interest is the establishment of the shrine of Tulaja mata or Taleju ma, a Shakti Goddess—held in high esteem by the Newars (of Nepal)—who later became the titular deity of the Malla (Newar) dynasty of Kantipur (Kathmandu) in the 17th century".[9]

Until 1774 AD., the eastern Terai was ruled by the Sen Kings of Makwanpur, who had Maithili as their national language. In 1657 AD., the King of Makwanpur donated a hundred acres of land to Chaturbhujgiri at Janakpur and built several temples there. This temple town of Janakpur later drew many patrons from India as well as Nepal.[10]

Prithvi Narayan Shah, attacked the Sen King in 1774. By 1775, the eastern as well as central region of the Terai was conquered. Furthermore, the larger portions of the western region of the Terai were also annexed to the territory of Nepal by 1789.[11]

The Terai region, whether in possession of the Sen or Shah kings, was under the suzerainty of the 'Saltanat' of Mughul emperors and the East India Company (Calcutta) of India and, therefore, they had to pay rent for using the resources of this region. It is to be noted that following the conquest of Makwanpur, the Gurkhas claimed the cultivated lowlands upon the payment to the British Government of the same tribute as was hitherto being paid by the Raja of Makwanpur. The British Government had no objection to this offer. Accordingly, for thirty years the Gurkhas had to pay large sized elephants to the British Government as a tribute for these lands annually. It was only by Article 7 of the Treaty of 1801 that the provision of paying tribute was annulled.[12] (Appendix III).

Subsequently, during the war between Nepal and the British East India Company in 1814-16, Nepal lost its entire Terai region. During the Treaty of Sugouli in 1815, Nepal had to relinquish all its land east of the Mechi river and west of Mahakali river and these rivers were fixed as Nepal's boundaries (Appendix IV). Following the pledge of loyalty to the British, Nepal was again allowed to regain its authority on the eastern Terai one year after the Sugouli Treaty (Appendix V). Later on, by virtue of helping the British to suppress the Sepoy Mutiny in India in 1857-58, Jang Bahadur, in compliance with the Treaty in 1860, received back in return a few districts of the western Terai called Naya Muluk (Appendix VII). Earlier, these districts of Nepal were annexed by the British.[13]

Forests

Until the middle of the 20th century, the Terai region was mostly covered with thick forests. Valuable trees, such as sal, sisso, khair, siri, semal, karma, bamboo, etc. existed there. Besides, all sorts of herbs were found. Kings and emperors in all ages used to pay visits to the Terai for hunting; as all sorts of animals including lions, tigers, elephants, rhinoceroses, deer and antelopes were available there. Crocodiles were also available.[14] But now there is hardly any thick forest left in the Terai except in the national parks. The forest in this region is, unprotected and it is being depleted on a huge scale, which has now been a great concern of the government and NGOs.

Population

Until 1954, the share of the Terai in the total population of Nepal was 35 percent which increased to 50 percent by the end of the 1980s. It is estimated to reach 57 percent in 2001 and 62 percent in 2011.

Estimates are that the number of Madheshi population is somewhat 7.5 million, which is approximately 40 percent of the total population of Nepal, viz. 18.9 million in 1990.[15] It is also being claimed by certain quarters that the share of the Madheshi people in the total population of the country is half.[16]

Notes

1. Thakur, Raghunath, *Madhesh Aur Uski Sanskriti,* (Hindi). Morang, 1959, p. 7.
2. Ibid., p. 10.
3. Ibid., p. 13.
4. "Nepal's Tarai: Backwater or New Frontier?", *Himal,* September/October, 1990, p. 6.
5. Bista, Dor Bahadur, *People of Nepal,* Ratna Pustak Bhandar, Kathmandu, 1987, p. 109.
6. Jha, Makhan, *The Sacred Complex in Janakpur,* United Publishers, Allahabad, 1971, pp. 5-6.
7. Thakur, Upendra, *History of Mithila,* Mithila Institute, Darbhanga, 1956, p. 234.
8. Ibid., pp. 282-85.
9. Ibid, p. 372.

10. Jha, No. 6, pp. 34-35.

11. Blaikie, Piers, Cameron, John and Seddon, David, *Nepal in Crisis: Growth and Stagnation at the Periphery*, Oxford University Press, Delhi, 1980, p. 28.

12. Aitchison, C.U. (Compiled), *A Collection of Treaties, Engagements and Sanads Relating to India and Neighbouring Countries*, (Vol. II), Superintendent Government Printing, Calcutta, 1909, p. 91.

13. Blaikie, No. 11, pp. 30-32.

14. Mishra, Hemant, "A Wild World That is No More", *Himal*, September/October 1990, pp. 14-15.

15. Parmanand, "The Indian Community in Nepal and the Nepalese Community in India: Their Socio-Cultural Problems", Paper submitted to an International Seminar on Indo-Nepal Relations: Anthroponomical and Geo-Economic Linkages, Centre for the Study of Nepal, Banaras Hindu University, Varanasi, March 24-26, 1990, p. 3.

16. Inaugural Speech of G.N. Singh on the Occasion of the Second National Convention of Nepal Sadbhavana Party held at Birgunj on April 17, 1993.

2

THE SOCIAL STRUCTURE

Background

In Nepal, the Terai region is rich in culture and tradition. The way of life the Madheshi people have adopted is in many ways different from that of the mountains and the hills. The caste system, language, dress, food habits and housing structure of these people are all distinct. Social harmony, especially in the rural areas, is almost unsurpassed. People share both joy and sorrow together forgetting caste consideration. Every person is tied up with others through the chain of social relations.

Caste System

In the Hindu religious text the Bhagavad Gita, Lord Krishna said that all the four castes - the Brahman, Kshatriya, Vaishya and Shudra were created by him on the basis of quality of jobs they were assigned to perform. By virtue of action called karma, one could achieve higher or lower status in the caste hierarchy.

Originally, the caste system was based on the principle of division of labour as it believed in specialization in one's own field. Accordingly, the Brahman represented the intellectual, the Kshatriya the warrior, the Vaishya the farmer and trader, and the Shudra the service class.

The caste system which has its roots in quality subsequently became associated with birth and lineage and, due to this the dynamism in the society, met with a setback. This was more true of the Hindu society, including that of the Terai.[1]

The four major castes (Brahman, Kshatriya, Vaishya, and Shudra) were gradually divided into many sub-castes. The new sub-caste includes Bhumihar treated on a par with the Brahman. The Rajput is regarded as Kshatriya. Another sub-caste, Kayastha, is given a place next to the Brahman and is assigned the job of keeping the accounts.

The sub-castes like Yadav, Mali (gardener), Amat, Koeeree, etc. are associated with agricultural production The other sub-castes, like the Suri, Teli (oil seller), Kanoo, Kalwar (wine seller), Rauniyar, Rastogi, Tamoli (betel seller), Mallah (fisherman), Halwai (confectioner) and Kathbaniya are engaged in business by tradition. Besides, Dhanuk, Kurmi Hajam (barber), Sonar (goldsmith), and Lohar (iron monger), Dhobi (washerman) and Chamar (performing leather work and also playing on flutes and beating drums) could be associated with the service class.

Khatabe or Kahar (who carry the bride/bridegroom on a "Palki," i.e. planquin) Musahar (who dig out rats from holes and eat them), Tatma and Dushad are by tradition agricultural labourers and they could be associated with the service class.

Mehatar (cleaning dirt) and Dom (providing fire during cremations) could be associated with the service class.

Marwari is also one of the Hindu sub-castes. By tradition the people of this sub-caste sell textile goods and now they are engaged in many industrial and trade activities.

Mention might also be made of Tharu, Rajbanshi, Gangai, Tajpuria, Satar, Danuwar and Bantar who in the past used to live as tribes in thick forests and were as farmers.[3] But they are no more primitive and tribal now.

They have adopted caste culture. Danuwars, for example, associate themselves with the royal Brahman class. They perform Hindu religious rites and worship Hindu gods and goddesses. Similarly, Rajbanshis claim to be Kshatriyas.

Of late, this age-old caste and sub-caste system appears to be slackening in social practice, especially in sharing food. The Muluki Ain (National Code) of 1963 has also formally outlawed any sort of discrimination on the basis of caste. However, the caste system still serves as a determinant in many aspects of life, especially poll campaign, marriage and caste-specific rituals.

The caste system has also shown its presence in the Muslim religious community, like Sheikh, Shaiyad, Dhuniya, Pathan and Julaha. However, this system is not as rigid among the Muslim community as their Hindu counterpart. Most of the people of the Muslim community serve as masons, tailors and butchers in the Terai.

Caste Groups in the 1991 Census

Since the government census did not specify the population figure on the basis of ethnicity/caste groups until 1981, it was not known as to what the exact population of the Madheshi community was in the total population of Nepal. It was only during the 1991 census that the population figure was presented on the basis of ethnic/caste groups. The following table shows that the Tharu has the largest population (6.46 percent) followed by Yadav (4.01 percent), Musalman (3.28 percent), Teli (1.35 percent), Chamar (1.01 percent), Koeeree (Kushawaha) (1.01 percent) and Brahman (1.01 percent). The table also shows that all the remaining Madheshi caste groups have population less than 1 percent.

However, the result of the 1991 census appears to be faulty because it failed to present the true size of population of the different Madheshi caste groups. For example, such caste groups, as Bhumihar, Amat, Mali, Kanoo,

Rauniyar, Rastogi, Tamoli, Kathbaniya, Hajam, Sonar, Lohar, Tajpuriya, Bantar, Tatma, Dom, Mehtar, etc. have not been represented in the census figures. It is for this reason that the population of the Madheshi community on the basis of the caste groups has been shown merely 26.75 percent (Table 2.1), which is grossly underenumerated.

Table 2.1: Percentage Distribution of Population by Caste Groups in the Terai

Caste/Ethnic Group	*Percent of the Total Population*
Tharu	6.46
Yadav	4.01
Musalman	3.28
Teli	1.35
Chamar	1.01
Koeeree (Kushawaha)	1.01
Brahman	1.01
Sudi/Kalwar	0.94
Kurmi	0.92
Musahar	0.75
Dhanuk	0.73
Baniya	0.51
Kewat	0.49
Dushadh	0.48
Mai ah	0.45
Rajbansi	0.42
Kanu	0.41
Dhobi	0.41
Khatway	0.34
Kayastha	0.32
Kumhar	0.31
Rajput	0.31
Danuwar	0.27
Halwai	0.24
Marwari	0.15
Gangai	0.08
Bangali	0.04
Shikh	0.04
Raute	0.01
TOTAL	26.75

Source: Central Bureau of Statistics: Four Monthly Statistical Bulletin (2049-50)

Art and Painting

Dance is an important part of social life in the Terai. Jhumar is one such dance performed by the women-folk during marriage ceremonies. Jhijhiya dance is performed by the women during the Dashami festival. Dom Kachha is in vogue in the society. Dance by the Natuwas is very common. The Natuwas are not women but men who dance in the guise of women.

Folksong of Salhesh or Lori is common among rural people. Women love singing in groups and they do so during marriages, festivals, and other such auspicious occasions.

Fine arts are also highly developed. The Kumhar caste of people, called *pandits,* make artistic tiles, utensils, idols of various gods and goddesses out of clay.

Painting has been part and parcel of the folk culture of the Terai. It is performed invariably by women-folk in eastern and central Terai. It has gained a universal reputation now in the name of "Janakpur" or "Mithila" painting.

Though paintings, by and large, are performed on walls (mural) and on the ground (aripana), they are also done on pottery, fans and earthen dishes. Recently, they are being performed on paper and clothes in view of their growing commercial values. Dr. Upendra Thakur writes about the women painters of Mithila, "[they]... are born 'Picassos'. What they could not do through a study of the alphabet, they do it through these paintings."[4]

There is hardly any school or college in the Terai where folk songs, arts or paintings are taught. It is all traditional flowing from one generation to the other spontaneously.

Additionally, women also make other artistic goods, which include terra-cotta figurines, sikki articles, embroidery, sujani, applique, doll-making (kaniya-putara in Maithili), etc.

Settlement Pattern

There are three types of house structure in the Terai: thatched huts, houses roofed by tiles, and concrete houses, depending upon the economic status of the people. Of all these three types of houses, the thatched huts arc most common. It is basically made of locally available materials like mud, bamboo, and wood, with a sloping roof of thatch. Usually, there is a courtyard in the centre of the more or less nucleated knots of these houses.

In most of the traditional houses in the rural areas, not much importance was given to ventilation or the toilets. But now on account of the rise in the level of consciousness people have started realizing the importance of ventilation. Yet toilets are, by and large, uncommon within the houses.

Dress/Attirc

The traditional common dress of most of the people in the Terai includes *dhoti, kurta* and *gamchha* for the men and *sari* and *blouse* for women. But in certain community, like Satar, men use merely *langoti,* which is just enough to cover certain parts of their bodies. This is also the case with such people as Musahars, Dushads, Doms, etc.

There is, however, a growing trend among the educated people to shift towards western dress, such as pants, shirts, etc, though the larger number of the Terai people, particularly the women-folk, have still preserved their traditional dress.

In certain communities, such as among the Tharu, the dress of a woman is *cholo* and *ghaghara/patuka*. In this context, mention needs to be made of the dress of a Rana Tharu woman, which is gorgeous and lasting. It takes at least six months for a woman to prepare one set of the dress for a Rana Tharu woman.

The *purdah* system, the tradition of keeping women in seclusion, is still practised, though in varying degrees.

Owing to this, the women do not move so freely out of their homes. This system is not as common among the hill women as the Madheshi women.

Most of the Madheshi Muslim women use the same attive as the Hindu women. Yet certain Muslim women can also be seen in burka, which is typically made to wrap the entire body except the eyes.

Women in the Terai have special attraction towards ornaments, which are made of gold and silver. It is from the head to foot that the women wear ornaments. In the middle of the head, they use mantikka. They use earrings, nose rings, neck rings and necklaces. They also use *ageli* on the wrists, *bichelli* on the elbows, and *pichheli* on the armpits. Likewise, they use *darkas* round their waist. *Kanda* and *payal* are used round the ankles. Besides, finger rings and toe rings are also used. Besides, *bulki* (worn in the nose), *hausli* (worn around the throat) and the like are still popular among the females. There are splendid designs of the ornaments.

During marriages, a bride is invariably given ornaments by the in-laws. Ornaments prove helpful to a family, especially during difficult days.

Major Festivals

The Terai is colourful round the year. Every month there is one festival or the other. The important festivals include *Makar Sankranti, Holi, Jurshital, Chaurchan, Durga Puja, Dipavali, Chhaith, Sama-Chakeva, Eid* and *Moharram.*

Makar Sankranti (January) is observed during the winter on January 14 to mark the change of season. People bathe in the early morning and offer rituals in the fire. They eat gur, til and *ghee* compulsorily apart from *khichari.* They also prepare different varieties of local sweets on this occasion.

Holi (February-March) is a colourful festival. People throw colours and colour powders on one another and rejoice. It is also a day to create social harmony. People forget the feeling of animosity and love one another. They consume sweets, meat and *bhang* (intoxicating item). Many of them sing, beat drums, dance and are merry.

Jurshital (March-April) is a very important festival in the Terai. This is the symbol of the beginning of the new year (Vikram Samvat) amid the spring season. In the early morning, the elders sprinkle water on the heads of the youth and bless them. There is also a system of pouring water in the roots of the mango trees. By tradition, people also coasume stale food items, which include *badi, bhat,* etc. in the Mithila region. This is the occasion when people throw mud on one another.

Chaurchan is the corrupt form of the Sanskrit word Chauth Chandra, meaning the fourth day of the lunar calender month of Bhadra (August- September). People worship the moon god and offer him different kinds of sweets. On the next day, God Ganesh, the symbol of good omen, is worshipped, especially by school children.

Durga Puja (September-October) is the most important festival. Idols of Goddess Durga are made in villages and towns. People staying outside return to their home during this period. Friends and relatives meet together. This festival, thus, creates social harmony. Durga is the symbol of divinity and she kills the powerful demons. Especially, the Brahmans recite Durga Pustak. The Tantriks try to achieve *siddhis* or enlightenment during ten days of Durga Puja through the recitation of mantras. Durga Puja begins on *Ghatasthapana* and ends on the tenth day called Vijaya Dashami. On the day of *Ghatasthapana,* people sow barley at sacred places in their homes and reap it on the day of Vijaya Dashami. It was on this day of Vijaya Dashami that Lord Ram got victory over the demon King Ravana during the Ramayana period.

Dipavali (October) is the festival of lights. It is also called Lakshmi Puja or Sukh Ratri. This is the occasion when people worship Goddess Lakshmi, the symbol of wealth and pleasure. People invariably clean their surroundings. They put lights all over their homes. Various delicious sweets and fruits are offered to Lakshmi. They also play with *Hukaloli*.

Chhaith (October-November) is another important festival in which Lord Surya, the sun god, is worshipped. It is unique that first of all the setting sun is worshipped and then the rising sun. Devotees offer various delicious items to the sun during the evening and morning in ponds and rivers.

Sama-Chekeva (November) is celebrated particularly in the Mithila region of the Terai following the *Chhaith* puja. The ladies make colourful toys and artistic figures, based on the earthen clay, jute, and sikki (grass). The earthenware figures include Sama (sister of Samba, son of Lord Krishna) and Chakeva (husband of Sama), Chugla (backbiter), Vrindavana (forest), Satbhaiya (seven rishis), etc. The story goes like this. Chudaka, called Chugla, reports to Krishna that Sama maintained illicit relations with seven rishis of Vrindavana. Upon this, Sama was cursed to become a bird and so were the seven rishis. At this, the husband, Chakeva, also opted to become a bird like his wife, Sama. Credit goes to Samba, the son of Lord Krishna, to help these birds to be transformed into human beings again by dint of his penance. This Pauranic story is commemorated each year by the ladies with the view that the innocent people should not fall victim of the backbiter in the society. Beautiful and colourful images of all these figures are made by the ladies and put on a plate-like basket called *changeri* in Maithili. The village ladies walk to their fields for fifteen nights continuously by carrying the *changeris* on their heads and singing songs, specially composed for this occasion. They also indulge in group dances and playful skits. Vrindavana is burnt. Face of Chugla is burnt and darkened. And finally on the full- moon night, the ladies place four-faced lamps in the field, exchange the *changeris* with other groups, and seek the assistance of their brothers to break the earthen images, including Sama and Chakeva before returning home.[5]

The Muslim community celebrates Eid and Muharram (Tajia). Many Hindus also join the Muslims during Tajia, especially in Western Terai.

Survey Results

During the field survey, information was collected about various aspects of the social life of the Madheshi community, which are described as follows:

Household Size

Table 2.2 indicates that 49 percent of the sample households in the Terai have 5 to 10 members; whereas 47 percent have 5 members, and the remaining 4 percent have more than 10 members. The average household size is 6.

Table 2.2: Household Size

Household Size	*Number of Households*	*Percentage*
Upto 5	467	47
5 to 10	494	49
Over 10	39	4
TOTAL	1000	100

Source: Field Survey, 1992

The sample survey exhibits a distinct trend towards the disintegration of joint families into nuclcar ones. As much as 82 percent of the total families are nuclear. The joint families constitute merely 18 percent The division of the families is not rated high in the traditional social structure. In the past, when the pressure on land and property was limited, it was not very difficult for many families to live together. But now the sub-division of land holding on the one, and poverty on the other, do not allow members to live together for long.

Male-Female and Dependency Ratio

Table 2.3 shows that the share of women in the total sample population is 47 percent, which is lower than the national average of 50 percent.[6] There are many factors responsible for this phenomenon. The desire for a son is very strong. As a result, parents have a tendency to limit the size of their family when their requirement for a son is fulfilled.

Abortion, though illegal, is practised on a limited scale. Gender test is not much known to common people. Yet on the basis of certain traditional beliefs and also by consulting doctors some women undergo abortions to avoid the possibility of daughters.

During the sample survey, 29 percent of the total households accepted that they discriminated against the girl child in providing food, clothing, health and education facilities. Similarly, 20 percent of the households expressed that they did not allow women to participate in the decision-making process.

The following table indicates that the dependency ratio is very high in the Terai. Active population between the age of 15 and 49 years account for only 49 percent of the total sample population. Dependency ratio (upto the age of 15 years and above 65 years) is 43 percent, which is high.

Table 2.3: Male -Female and Dependency Ratio

Age (Years)	*Male*	*Percentage*	*Female*	*Percentage*	*Total*	*Percentage*
Upto-5	485	15	491	18	976	17
5 - 10	496	16	448	16	944	16
10 - 15	337	11	217	8	554	9
15 -49	1492	48	1375	49	2867	49
49 -65	272	9	221	8	493	8
Above 65	35	1	34	1	69	1
TOTAL:	3117	100	2786	100	5903	100
Percentage	53	-	47	-	100	

Source: Field Survey, 1992.

Attitude Towards the Birth of the Girl Child

As shown in Table 2.4, the share of the sample households treating the birth of the girl child as normal and a boon is 78 percent and 15 percent, respectively. But the share of the households treating the birth of the girl child as a curse is merely 7 percent. This encouraging attitude towards the birth of the girl child is mainly due to the impact of modern education and growing awareness in the Terai.

It is not very difficult to understand why certain households take the birth of the girl child as a curse. A girl is expected to spend all her life after marriage at the house of her husband and, therefore, she cannot directly support her parents. Above all, the dowry problem adds to the misery of a family as under the social compulsion cash and kind have to be paid to the bridegroom.[7] This is one of the basic problems of indebtedness in the society. The amount received in the form of dowry is mostly used on unproductive purposes; like arranging feasts as well as purchasing luxurious items, including cycles, transistors, watchs, scooters, motor cycles, cars, etc.

During the sample survey, as much as 67 percent of the households accepted that they had the dowry system. Only 33 percent of the households disapproved of this practice. The amount of the dowry was hardly uniform and varied depending on the economic and social status of a family. On an average, Rs. 24,343 was spent on dowry at the time of a girl's marriage .

The Madheshi society is neck deep in dowry problem. It is a great burden on those whose sources of income are limited. Awareness against this social evil practice is lacking.

Table 2.4: Reaction About the Birth of a Girl Child

Categories	*Number of Households*	*Percent*
Boon	154	15
Normal	774	78
Curse	72	7
TOTAL	1000	100

Source: Field Survey, 1992.

Child Labour

Child labour is also a problem in the Terai. Hundreds of thousands of children below the age of fourteen are forced to work in miserable conditions in brick factories, agricultural fields, livestock farming, etc. Generally, they have to work between 12 and 15 hours a day. They suffer from certain diseases. Yet not much care is given to their health.

It is a violation of human rights to employ children since they lose an opportunity to develop themselves. It is shameful that the children have to work at a time when they are expected to play, learn, and enjoy life. During this early age, they are curious, active and full of hope. But these ill-fated children are devoid of all the charms of life, which they would never recover in their lifetime.

The children of today are the citizens of tomorrow. Survival, protection and development of the children are prerequisites for the country's future. It is, therefore, the responsibility of the state to ensure that the children are not deprived of the basic human rights.

Undoubtedly, the legislation, like the Nepali Labour Act 1992, has been made to address to the problems of child labour. The Act strongly opposes the employment of children below the age of fourteen years in a factory as well as in night work. But the law has not yet been very effective.

The Government of Nepal has also endorsed the World Summit Declaration and Plan of Action for the survival, development and protection of children for the 1990s on the principle of "Children First". It is also committed to implement the National Plan of Action for children based on the Goals for Children and Development for the 1990s, which includes reduction of malnutrition; universal access to safe drinking water and to sanitary means of excreta disposal; universal access to basic education; and protection of children in especially difficult circumstances. In practice, however, no substantial effort has been made to achieve the Goals for Children and Development for the 1990s.

Education Status

Table 2.5 indicates that 51 percent of the total sample size of population are illiterate. In other words, literate and educated people account for 49 percent. The literacy percentage in the Terai is higher than that of the national average of 41 percent[8].

The table also shows that the literacy rate is higher for males and lower for females, viz. 63 percent and 33 percent, respectively.

Table 2.5: Education Status

Education Level	*Male*	*Percentage*	*Female*	*Percentage*	*Total*	*Percentage*
Illiterate	1140	37.0	1872	67.0	3012	51.0
Primary	1051	34.0	610	22.0	1661	28.0
Middle	426	14.0	1%	7.0	622	11.0
Secondary	289	9.0	80	3.0	369	6.0
Intermediate	127	4.0	18	0.6	145	3.0
Bachelor	73	2.0	10	0.3	83	1.0
Masters & Above	11	0.3	-	-	11	0.3
TOTAL:	3117	100.0	2786	100.0	5903	100.0

Source: Field Survey, 1992

In the Terai, 28 percent of the people received primary, 11 percent middle, 6 percent secondary, 3 percent intermediate, 1 percent bachelor, and only 0.3 percent masters and above level education. It is to be noted that the share of the people receiving masters level education is marginal, which is also due to the lack of university in the Terai.

Marriage and Marriageable Age

In the Terai, marriage is universal and it is generally arranged. In certain castes, a woman cannot even think of remarriage no matter whether there is a proper matching or not. Even if a girl becomes a widow in her childhood or youth, she is not permitted by the social customs to remarry. However, such a compulsion does not exist for a man. He can easily remarry a woman after becoming a widower. The Brahman, Kayastha and Rajput, for example, are such castes where remarriage of the woman is prohibited.

The case of re-marriage or divorce does not reach the court of law. Inter-community marriage is a rare phenomenon. The survey result shows that 99 percent of the sample households have had intra-community marriages. Only 1 percent of the households reported the case of inter-community marriage, especially between the Madheshi and hill people.

Inter-caste marriage is not allowed even within the Madheshi community. A Brahman would marry only in the Brahman family, and so will the Kayastha, Musahar, Tatama, Khatabe, Chamar or Dom.

The Terai community is generally endogamous. Even within the same caste, a particular kind of caste does not marry with the same nature of another caste. For example, the Maithil Brahman does not marry in the family of Saraswat or Kankubj Brahman and similarly, the Karna Kayastha does not marry in the family of Srivastava. Confinement of the marriage within the same group of caste is also one of the reasons of the growing dowry system in the Terai as it restricts the choice.

Moreover, within the same caste, such as Brahman, Kayastha or Yadav, marriage does not so frequently occur between the different groups. For example, among the Brahmans the *Srotriyas* and *Yogas* hesitate to marry the *Jaibars* and among the Yadavs the *Kishanauts* hesitate to marry the *Majharauts,* the reason being that the *Srotriyas* or *Yogas* regard themselves superior to the *Jaibars* and so do the *Kishanauts* compared to the *Majharauts.*

Marriage is also prohibited within the same Gotra in the same caste. Though being a Brahman, a Kashyap Gotra boy does not marry another Kashyap Gotra girl and so is the situation in Sandilya, Vatsya and other Gotras.

There is a system of maintaining genealogical records or what is called "Panjiprabandha" among the Maithil Brahman and Karna Kayastha. On this basis, marriage is avoided between the boy and girl upto five generations on the mother's side and seven generations on the father's side.

Though marriage is universal, the *sadhus* or saints are expected to maintain celibacy throughout their life. Cases of women abstaining from marriage and leading the life of nuns right from their birth is rare. It is only at an advanced age and that too after becoming widows that certain women turn into nuns, who are called *mairams.*

Table 2.6 presents that 47 percent of people are married by the age of 15. Half of the total population (50 percent) get married between the age of 15 and 25. Persons marrying between the age of 25 and 30 account for only 3 percent. Marriage above the age of 30 years is non-existent.

Lack of awareness and illiteracy are the two main factors for child or early marriage. With the growth in the literacy rate, the marriageable age has been increasing.

Table 2.6: Marriageable Age

Marriage Age	*Number of Persons*	*Percentage*
Upto- 15	1261	47
15 - 25	1344	50
25 - 30	88	3
Above 30	0	0
Total	2693	100

Source: Field Survey, 1992

Civil Position

Table 2.7 indicates that the share of married people in the total sample population is 49 percent. Nearly 48 percent people are unmarried. Those who are widows/ widowers account for merely 3 percent of the total sample population.

The table also shows that a little over half of the women (52 percent) are married, while the share of the married men is less, i.e. 45 percent. This is due to the fact that the women get married earlier than the men and also that polygamy is allowed especially for a man without a son. Divorce is, however, very unusual in this community.

Table 2.7: Civil Position

Categories	*Male*	*Percentage*	*Female*	*Percentage*	*Total*	*Percentage*
Unmarried	1629	52	1241	45	2870	48
Married	1426	46	1446	52	2872	49
Remarried	1	0	0	0	1	0
Divorced	0	0	0	0	0	0
Widows/ Widowers	61	2	99	4	160	3
Total	3117	100	2786	100	5903	100

Source: Field Survey, 1992.

Religion

According to Table 2.8, the share of the Hindus in the total sample households is 91 percent followed by Muslims (8 percent) and others (1 percent). The Terai region is noted for maintaining social harmony among different religious groups.

Table 2.8: Religion

Religion	*Number of Households*	*Percentage*
Hindu	908	91
Muslim	81	8
Others	11	1
TOTAL	1000	100

Source: Field Survey, 1992.

Note: Others include Sikh, Buddhists, etc.

Conclusion

It is good that the Terai community has been preserving its traditional culture. Yet many evil practices, such as casteism, dowry system, discrimination against women, child marriage, etc. have become closely linked to the traditional social system. These evils will make the society weaker. Awareness, therefore, has to be created against these social practices, for which education is most essential.

There is a great potentiality for achieving universal literacy and creating mass education in the Terai considering the development of infrastructural facilities there. The government and other concerned organizations should accord maximum priority to the expansion of educational facilities in this region so that it could serve as a model for other regions of Nepal too. Problems, like casteism, dowry system, discrimination against the girl child, and child marriage are likely to be reduced by educating the Terai community properly.

Notes

1. Sharma, Ram Prakash, *History of Mithila,* Kameshwar Singh Darbhanga Sanskrit Vishwavidyalaya, Durbhanga, 1979, p. 549.
2. Prasad, Ramashish, *The Plains People,* September/ October 1990, p. 10.
3. Budhamagar, Harkha Bahadur, *Kirat Bansh Ra Magarharu,* (Nepali), Smt. Unnati Bohara, Laliipur, p.20.
4. Thakur, Upendra, *Madhubani Painting,* Abhivav Publications, New Delhi, (no date), p.55.
5. Ibid., pp. 35-36.
6. His Majesty's Government of Nepal, National Planning Commission Secretariat, *Four Monthly Statistical Bulletins, (Nepali),* (Nepali, Marg-Falgun), 1993, Kathmandu, p.37.
7. Acharya, Meena, *The Maithili Women of Sirsia,* CEDA, Kathmandu, 1981, pp. 53-75.
8. HMG/N, No. 6, p. 39.

3

THE LANGUAGE ISSUE

Introduction

The language in a country could be constructive or destructive. If properly handled, it can play a dynamic role in integrating a nation; if not, it may prove disruptive. Countries like Switzerland and Canada are united because of their liberal language policy. On the other hand, Pakistan disintegrated in 1971 because of the forceful imposition of Urdu over the Bengali people in East Pakistan. Language is also one of the factors of rift between the Tamil and Singhali speaking-population in Sri Lanka.[1] In Nepal, as many as 44 languages/dialects are spoken. As in the hills, many languages/dialects like Maithili, Awadhi, Bhojpuri, Hindi, Rajbanshi, Santhali, Satar, etc., are spoken by the Madheshi community in the Terai. Maithili is a dominant language in the Eastern Terai, Bhojpuri in the Mid-Terai and Awadhi in the Western Terai. Hindi, of course, serves as a lingua franca among the Madheshi people from the Mechi river in the east to the Mahakali river in the west.

Specifically, Maithili is a dominant language in Morang, Sunsari, Saptari, Sirha, Dhanusha, Mahottari, Sarlahi, and Rauthat. Influence of Maithili in Jhapa, Bara and Parsa is partial. In Jhapa, apart from Maithili such local dialects as Rajbanshi and Satar are also spoken. Bhojpuri is a dominant language in districts like Bara, Parsa, Chitwan and Nawalparasi districts. Awadhi is spoken mainly in districts like Rupandehi, Kapilvastu, Banke, Bardia, Kailali and Kanchanpur.[2]

The languages spoken in the Terai functioned as the languages of the court and culture of the Newar Kings, along with the Tibeto-Burman dialect in Kathmandu Valley. The court language of Patan in Kathmandu Valley was not Khasa but closely allied to Maithili in 1650 AD. Similarly, Awadhi, Maithili and Bengali were used as languages of culture in the court of Newari kings. A number of dramas were written in these languages in Nepal right down to the middle of the 18th century.[3]

Language Controversy

During the ancient period, language was not at all a problem in Nepal. Sanskrit was acknowledged as the source of all knowledge. In the medieval period, apart from Newari, Maithili served as an influential language of the court (during the reign of the Malla kings in Kathmandu Valley). Outside the Kathmandu Valley, the small principalities used Maithili, Awadhi, Bhojapuri and Hindi as their court languages.

After the unification of Nepal during the reign of King Prithvi Narayan Shah, the administrative function of the state was carried out in local languages, including Hindi. The early kings of the Shah dynasty used Nepali and Hindi as the languages of the state. Besides, Sanskrit and English were also important. Also, during the 104-year-old rule of the Ranas, language was not an issue as both the Hindi and Nepali were given importance. Till 1951, Hindi continued to be used as the medium of instruction and Nepali was the language of administration in Nepal.[4]

The language controversy arose following the political change in 1951. The National Education Planning Commission (NEPC) was established in 1954 and came out with its report in 1956. The NEPC recommended that Nepali should be the medium of instruction in all the grades of school education. It was also recommended that no language other than Nepali be taught even optionally at primary school, for that would hinder the teaching of Nepali.[5] The adoption of Nepali as the sole medium of instruction intended to avoid the cost of preparing textbooks in many languages. It was claimed that Nepali, the national language, had more affinity with Hindi than any other local language. Besides, it was also emphasized that no truly Hindi-speaking people inhabited any part of the country.[6]

In order to justify the introduction of Nepali as the medium of education, the number of Nepali-speaking population was over-enumerated in the census reports. Frederich H. Gaige in his book *Regionalism and National Unity in Nepal* cited many examples to show how the number of Nepali- speaking population was over-enumerated and that of the non-Nepali speaking population under-enumerated. Gaige states, "Pro-Nepali census administrators in Kathmandu have used a broad definition for Nepali, including in the Nepali category speakers of various dialects and perhaps also some other languages, thus inflating the figures so that Nepali could be claimed as the mother tongue of a majority of the population. For example, in Baitadi and Dandeldhura, districts in the far-western hills bordering on the Kumaon region of India, the inhabitants are enumerated as Nepali-speakers, despite the fact that Nepali-speaking district administrators deputed from Kathmandu do not understand much of the local language. It appears that the people of Baitadi and Dandeldhura speak Kumaun, the language of 96 percent of the people in the contiguous Indian hill district of Almora".[7]

If Gaige's views are accepted, it becomes obvious that the share of Nepali-speaking people in the total population of the country is not 53 percent, as the 1991 census reports,[8] but lower.

It was unfair to ban all the options of studying language/languages other than Nepali. The NEPC clearly recommended,"...no other language should be taught, even optionally, in the primary school because: few children will have need for them, they would hinder the teaching of Nepali".[9] At a time when the larger segments of the illiterate common masses of the population needed education in their mother tongues, it was an act to deprive them of their rights so as to ignore their interests. It was also fallacious to assume that the children in the country needed no language/languages other than Nepali. Also, in the name of avoiding preparation of textbooks in many languages, the growth of different mother tongues was obstructed owing to lack of opportunity to use them.

The NPEC wrongly claimed that no language had as much affinity with Hindi as Nepali and on this ground the imposition of Nepali was justified. This claim, however, cannot serve as justification for denying the role of Hindi in the educational institutions.

Language Movement

Ever since the Terai Congress (TC) was established in 1951, it gave a call for the recognition of Hindi as a second national language of Nepal. The Hindi movement took a dramatic turn in 1956 when the K.I. Singh government articulated to challenged the role of this language by issuing a directive.

Various public meetings and demonstrations were organized in different parts of the Terai in protest against the removal of Hindi from the school education. "Save Hindi" campaigns and "Save Hindi" committees were formed in a number of towns of the Terai in support of Hindi.[10] Interestingly enough, the campaign initiated by TC in support of Hindi got support from other national parties as well, like the Nepali Congress (NC), the Communist Party of Nepal (CPN), the United Democratic Party (UDP) and the Praja Parishad (PP).[11]

In 1957, Vedananda Jha, the president of TC, stated, "We will not allow the removal of Hindi from the medium of education. We will make all the sacrifices for this. The Terai people will never tolerate any insult to Hindi. If the people in the Terai remain silent today, Hindi will have very bad days...".[12] Kashi Prasad Srivastava, General Secretary of the ruling party UDP, at one of the meetings in Rajbiraj, said,"It is our weakness that the government has dared to impose Nepali as a medium of instruction on us. We have to be united on the issue of Hindi. It will be a blunder if we fail to do so. The language of the Terai is Hindi and it is my conviction that the language of the court in the Terai should be Hindi as well".[13] Similarly, the secretary of the Hindi Sahitya Parishad (Birgunj) expressed, "The denial of Hindi language means disrespect of the Terai people as well as the Hindi-speaking people living in other parts of the country. The Hindi-speaking population will never accept this unjustified decision of the government".[14] It was also added that the removal of Hindi was against the spirit of national integration as it was expected to create dissension between the Madheshi and hill people in Nepal.[15]

In 1957, Matrika Prasad Koirala said, "The imposition of Nepali as a medium of instruction in school education will aggravate rather than resolve the problem".[16] Surya Prasad Upadhyaya also subscribed to almost similar views about the language issue.

In 1957, the nation was obviously divided into pro-Hindi and anti-Hindi factions. The government of Nepal sided with the anti-Hindi faction. In one of the press communiques, it charged the pro-Hindi supporters as 'vested interests' with narrow outlook.

The rigid stand taken by the government in regard to the language issue resulted in protests at several places. At the end of October, 1957, the government banned all sorts of protests against the language directive. But this could not stop the zeal of the Hindi supporters. An ultimatum was served by the Birgunj Save Hindi Committee that the directive should be withdrawn by November 11, 1957; failing to do so would result in launching a struggle. But the government turned a deaf ear to this ultimatum. When the deadline of the ultimatum expired, there were meetings, protest marches and strikes in Biratnagar, Gaur, Rajbiraj and Janakpur. The dismissal of the K.I. Singh government by King Mahendra on November 14, 1957 could not pacify the sentiments of pro-Hindi protestors. On November 19, 1957, there were incidents of street fighting and looting in Biratnagar when the processions led by local Save Hindi Committee and Nepali Pracharini Sabha clashed with one another.[17]

In January 1958, the Ministry of Education under King Mahendra issued a second directive and tried to divert the attention of the public from the language controversy. For this, he announced a Royal Proclamation and fixed the date of the national election in February 1959.

In this election, the NC won a majority of seats in the parliament. The B.P. Koirala government allowed Hindi to remain as a medium of instruction from the primary to the university level education. Apart from Nepali, such local languages, as Hindi, Maithili and Newari were also taught in the schools. Hindi was also the language of the parliament at that time.

When the democratically elected government of B.P. Koirala was dissolved in 1960, Hindi was abolished as a medium of instruction at school as well as college level education by the Panchayat regime. Additionally, Hindi was declared as a foreign language.

All the branches of the Nepal-India Cultural Centre were closed in the initial years of the Panchayat regime. The Centre was established in 1950 with its head office in Kathmandu and branches in such towns of the Terai, as

Biratnagar, Birgunj and Nepalgunj. Books and literature, especially in Hindi, used to be available at these branches.

The New Education Plan (NEP) introduced in 1971 discouraged education in Hindi medium further.[18] The school curricula made provisions for students to study Hindi in standards 9 and 10 as an optional subject; however, there was no teacher made available to teach this language. As a result, the teaching of Hindi remained sidetracked.

Derecognition of Local Languages

The Marichman Singh government during the end of the Panchayat system even derecognized the degree of M.A. in Hindi, Maithili and Newari as a basis of promotion. All the languages other than Nepali and English were derecognized by the Public Service Commission. Sajha Prakashan has also been biased for not publishing books in these languages. Even at the Royal Nepal Academy, not much importance is being given to the development of these languages and their literature as well as the scholars specialized in them, though it has been making tall claims about its efforts in this regard.

During the Panchayat regime, an institution devoted to the cause of Hindi literature was discouraged by all means. Similarly, even the publication of newspaper in Hindi was discouraged. News bulletins on Radio Nepal in Hindi and Newari were also stopped.

Language Policy of the Democratic Government

Following the restoration of democracy in 1990, the coalition government resumed news bulletins in Hindi and Newari from Radio Nepal. Since January 1, 1993, the news bulletin in Maithili has also been started. Furthermore, Radio Nepal is likely to begin broadcasts on the second channel with an objective to organize programmes among various ethnic groups and communities speaking different languages in the country. This is, indeed, a marked departure.

Yet the demand of the parliamentarians to allow them

to speak in their native languages was not allowed in the beginning.

A ridiculous situation in the case of the language issue arose at the very first session of the newly elected parliament in 1991. Khalil Miyan, the oldest member of the parliament, uttered some rulings in his usual Hindi language while administering the oath to other members. This was enough for certain MPs to oppose this unconscious use of Hindi. Some Nepali newspapers also highlighted this "unholy" fault of the use of Hindi in their headlines.

Questions were raised in the parliament that if the Prime Minister of the country could deliver speeches in Hindi when he visited the Terai districts, there was no sense in restricting the representatives of the Terai from using this language in parliament. Besides, issues were also raised that it was untenable to deny the use of Hindi in the parliament at a time when the chairman of the National Assembly gave a ruling against the use of Hindi in no language other than Hindi itself.[19]

It was over two months of untiring efforts that Rameshwar Yadav, member of Nepal Sadbhavana Party (NSP), was allowed to speak in Hindi at the first National Assembly in 1991. The NSP leaders like G. N. Singh, Hridayesh Tripathi and the others also made efforts to secure the recognition of Hindi as one of the languages of the House of Representatives. There were frequent rulings against the use of Hindi in both the National Assembly and House of Representatives before this language could be recognized.[20]

On the success of getting Hindi recognized as one of the languages of parliament, Rameshwar Yadav stated in the National Assembly, "I had promised my people that I would keep their dress, language and culture intact and, accordingly, I have been speaking Hindi in the parliament".[21]

However, it would be wrong to assume that the leaders of the NSP alone supported the cause of Hindi in the parliament. Certain leaders of NC and other political parties also backed NSP's demand of allowing the use of Hindi in the parliament. Such MPs as Suresh Malla of NC and Gopal Shakya of the Communist Party of Nepal (United Marxist-Leninist) (CPN, UML) also supported the move of the pro-Hindi MPs in the parliament.[22]

Another milestone was added in the field of language policy in the third parliamentary session. On July 7, 1992, Mahanta Thakur, Deputy Speaker of the House of Representatives, gave a historic ruling under Article 62 of the Constitution that the parliamentarians could use their native languages apart from the national language in discussions in the House. While giving this ruling, he added,"the Constitution has allowed full freedom for the parliamentarians to use their respective mother tongues except for the ministers, who will use the national language, and for government purposes and parliamentary notices" [23] This decision was highly applauded. Following this decision Seikh Idris, a Madheshi MP. of the ruling NC, spoke in Urdu in the parliament Similarly, Padma Ratna Tuladhar, CPN (UML), also expressed his views in Newari in the parliament.[24]

Status of Hindi

Despite the opposition to Hindi, this language is popular both among the Madheshi and non-Madheshi people in Nepal. People stand in queues for hours to buy ticket for Hindi films at the cinema halls in Kathmandu Valley as well as in other parts of the country. No Nepali stands in the queue for such a long time to get ticket of films at the cinema halls in language/languages other than Hindi.

Hindi papers, magazines, etc. are sold in Nepal more than the Nepali ones. It is the Hindi books that are read more than books in any other languages in libraries. Bookstores in the streets of Kathmandu display the banners inscribing "Get Hindi Novels on Hire Here".

Hindi TV. and radio programmes are also quite popular in Nepal. More than this, each year thousands of students receive education through the Hindi medium from Indian universities.[25] Additionally, a large number of people who go to India for employment also learn Hindi. The impact of all these activities is that the common Nepalese people have become quite familiar with the use of Hindi.

All the major languages of Nepal, such as Maithili, Bhojpuru, Awadhi and Nepali are the real sister languages of Hindi. Like Hindi, all these languages of Nepal share the same script, almost the same nature of words and uniformity in grammar.

Apart from the Nepali-speaking population, the Newars, speaking Tibeto-Burman language, and other ethnic groups in the hill region of Nepal also understand Hindi and use it as a lingua franca while communicating with other communities.[26]

Whatever superiority that Hindi maintains is due to the linguistic necessity and historical acceptance of it as a lingua franca in the greater Hindi zone of North India and Nepal Terai. During the last one thousand years, many languages of this greater Hindi zone climbed to the position of a central language or lingua franca due to their literary importance. For example, Rajasthani, Braja, Awadhi, Khariboli and even Maithili remained literary lingua francas of this zone at different periods of history and they were given almost the same importance as Hindi in the history of literature. Finally, this position of lingua franca was acquired by the Khariboli, a dialect spoken around Delhi. However, the standard Hindi has a synthetic character and, therefore, it includes features of all its sister languages.

Language Politics in the Census Reports

Nowhere outside India, are there as many Hindi speakers as in Nepal.[27] Yet, in the early 1950s, views were expressed by certain quarters that Hindi was spoken nowhere in the Terai. On the contrary, Vedananda Jha, the leader of TC, claimed that Hindi was the language of four million Madheshi people. But both these estimates were based on the personal estimates rather than on any census report. Information about the mother tongues were collected during the Census survey in 1952-54 but its report was not published till 1958.

Language data when published in 1958 created a controversy. Only 3 percent of the total population of Nepal, according to the census figure of 1952-54, had Hindi as their mother tongue. The number of Hindi speakers was further reduced from 80,181 in 1952-54 to 2,867 in the 1961 census. And surprisingly, no mention of Hindi-speaking population was made in the census reports of 1971 and 1981.

As regards the removal of Hindi from the census reports, Richard Burghart commented,"The absence of Hindi, the national language of India, from within the Kingdom of Nepal has been used by the Nepalese government as a means of affirming its cultural difference from India".[28] Frederich H. Gaige maintains that the members of Kathmandu's governing elite have a feeling that Hindi is the symbol of the Madheshi community's resistance to the hill culture. It may be for this reason that the number of Hindi speakers was deliberately distorted. In this context, Gaige adds, "at least 63 percent of the terai population spoke Hindi as either a first or second language in 1961. It is doubtful that this percentage has declined since 1961, given the growing commercial contacts between the Terai and India."[29]

In 1971 and the following census report, the word Hindi was struck off and was replaced by such other languages, as Rajbanshi, Danuwar and Tharu, on top of the three main languages of the Terai, viz. Maithili, Bhojpuri and Awadhi. Initially, such words, like 'Maithili Tharu', 'Bhojpuri Tharu' and 'Awadhi Tharu' were superfluously added. Subsequently, a separate word 'Tharu language' came into vogue.

An effort is being made by certain sections to prove that 'Tharu' is a language different from Maithili, Bhojpuri and Awadhi. But in his language survey, Grierson reveals that there is no such thing as the 'Tharu' language.[30] Suniti Kumar Chaterjee supports this view.[31] Furthermore, Krishna Chandra Mishra also holds that the Tharus do not have any language of their own from the Mechi river in the east to the Mahakali river in the west.

In fact, the Tharus have the same roots as the other Madheshis. If at all the 'Tharu' is a language, it is a dialect of Maithili, Bhojpuri or Awadhi. The people of this community speak the language as spoken in their geographical surroundings. For example, the Tharus in the Maithili-speaking area speak Maithili; the Tharus in Bhojpuri-speaking area speak Bhojpuri; and the Tharus in the Awadhi-speaking area speak Awadhi. What purpose does the new word Tharu language serve? Perhaps one of its objectives may be to show that the Tharus are different from the rest of the Madheshi community, which it is not. No one can believe that the Tharus between the Mechi river in the east and the Mahakali river in the west speak only one so-called Tharu language; while the other Madheshis in this vast geographical region speak different languages, such as Maithili, Bhojpuri and Awadhi.

Growth of Hindi

In fact, Hindi is not competitive but complementary to the growth of its sister languages, like Nepali, Maithili, Bhojpuri and Awadhi. Hindi is capable enough to enrich all these languages. Similarly, the development of Nepali, Maithili, Bhojpuri and Awadhi may also help the growth of Hindi.

For Nepal, Hindi is much more essential than English. English is understood by the elite whose share in the total population of the country is merely 0.03 percent. But the number of Hindi-speaking population in Nepal is in millions. And since millions of Nepalese have to speak Hindi in Nepal and also in India to settle matters related to education, service, business, etc., it is certainly not in Nepal's interests to accord step brotherly treatment to Hindi. "When the learning of English is encouraged at every step, there is no sense in discouraging Hindi. We feel it easier to speak Hindi than any other language", says Bhadrakali Mishra, the Chairman of Raj Parishad.

In view of the importance of Hindi as a link language between the people of the Terai and the hills, as well as between the people of Nepal and India, certain intellectuals contributed significantly to the growth of Hindi by writing books, editing newspapers, etc.

Chandra Lai Jha, the editor of *Nepal Times*, published his newspaper in 1957-58 in Hindi. The language of this paper changed from Hindi to Nepali only later on. In 1958, Uma Kant Das started the publication of a daily newspaper *Nepali* in Hindi which is now being published under the editorship of Vijay Kumar Das. Nepali is the only paper which had an uninterrupted publication even during the Panchayat system, when the administration was very hard on Hindi. Likewise, the Central Department of Hindi started the publication of an annual journal called *Sahitya Lok* in Hindi some ten years ago.

Immediately after the fall of the Panchayat system in 1990, Sukheshwar Pathak changed the language of his weekly newspaper *Vishleshan* from Nepali to Hindi. *Nava Nepal*, a standard Hindi monthly magazine edited by Krishna Chandra Mishra, had also established a record in critical journalism in Nepal in 1990. Yet it was unfortunate that this magazine could not continue after four issues.

Ajay Kumar Mishra established a branch of an international organization called Vishwo Hindi Prachar-Prasar Parishad at Janakpur in early 1992. One of the basic objectives of this organization is to give publicity to Hindi and also to organize the Fifth International Hindi Conference at Janakpur.[32]

Mother Tongues and the Constitution

Even during the Panchayat regime, some Madheshi intellectuals raised the demand in favour of having education in their mother tongues. Following the restoration of democracy in 1990, they became vocal. They want education upto the primary level in their mother tongues. Such demands were also placed before the Constitution Reform Commission after the political change in 1990.

The Constitution of the Kingdom of Nepal (1990) accepted that all the languages spoken as mother tongues in Nepal would be treated as national languages. In Article 18 of the Fundamental Rights of the Constitution, it is clearly stated, "(1) Each community residing within the Kingdom of Nepal shall have the right to preserve and promote its language, script and culture; [and] (2) Each community shall have the right to operate schools up to the primary level in its own mother tongue for imparting education to its children".[33] However, the Constitution is not clear as to how these national languages will be promoted. There is hardly any guarantee of support from the state for their development.[34] Recently the Minister of Education has expressed a desire to set up a national language council to promote the languages of Nepal and use them as the medium of primary education.

Survey Result

In order to examine the language issue, a survey was conducted in the sample districts of the Terai. Nearly 99 percent of the sample households reported that they had no access to education in their mother tongues. Of the sample households, 97 percent preferred primary level education in their mother tongues, such as, Hindi, Maithili, Bhojpuri and Awadhi.

First Language

Table 3.1 presents the list of first languages spoken by the sample households. Maithili is found to be the first language of 37 percent of the total sample households, followed by Awadhi (26 percent), Hindi (20 percent), Bhojpuri (13 percent); and Nepali (4 percent). As a first language, Hindi holds third place in the Terai next to Maithili and Awadhi.

Table 3.1: List of First Language

Language	*Number of Households*	*Percentage*
Maithili	371	37
Awadhi	258	26
Hindi	201	20
Bhojpuri	134	13
Nepali	36	4
TOTAL	1000	100

Source: Field Survey, 1992.

Distortion of Data in the 1991 Census

The following table which is based on the 1991 census shows that of the total population of Nepal the share of those having Maithili as their mother tongue accounts for 12 percent followed by Bhojpuri (7 percent), Tharu (5 percent), Awadhi (2 percent), Urdu (1 percent), Hindi (1 percent) and others (1 percent).

The figures presented in the table appear to be unrealistic in the sense that they are under-enumerated. On the basis of the mother tongue, the share of the

Madheshi community in the total population of the country is found to be merely 29 percent.

About 5 percent of the total population of Nepal is shown to have been speaking Tharu language, when there is no such language as "Tharu' anywhere in the Terai.

Table 3.2: Mother Tongues of the Madheshi Community

Mother Tongues	*As % of total Population of Nepal*
Maithili	12
Bhojpuri	7
Tharu	5
Awadhi	2
Urdu	1
Hindi	1
Others	1
Total	29

Source: 1. Population Census 1991 (based on 10 percent sampling of the total census figures).

2. *Four Monthly Statistical Bulletin (Marg-Falgun, 2049-50)*

Note: Others include Bengali (0.12%, Danuwar (0.12%), Satar (0.11%), Marwari (0.08%) and Dhimal (0.05%), Santhal (0.03%)

Link Language

According to Table 3.3, 81 percent of the Terai households accept Hindi as a link language followed by Awadhi (9 percent), Maithili (5 percent), Nepali (3 percent), and Bhojpuri (2 percent). Hindi is the only language, which the majority of the Madheshi households use as a link language within their community, as well as with the people of the Nepalese hills and people of India.

Table 3.3: Attitude Towards the Link Language

Language	*Number of Households*	*Percentage*
Hindi	810	81
Awadhi	85	9
Maithili	46	5
Nepali	28	3
Bhojpuri	15	2
Total	1000	100

Source: Field Survey, 1992.

National Language

The attitude of the Madheshi people appears to be somewhat different towards the national language from that of the link language. Table 3.4 shows that of the total sample households, 48 percent want Nepali to remain as the national language of Nepal; followed by Hindi (44 percent), Maithili (6 percent), and Awadhi (2 percent).

Table 3.4: Attitude Towards the National Language

Language	*Numberof Households*	*Percenetage*
Nepali	479	48
Hindi	437	44
Maithili	59	6
Awadhi	23	2
Bhojpuri	2	0
Total	1000	100

Source: Field Survey, 1992.

Conclusion

The state needs to be liberal in promoting different languages spoken in the Terai region. Growth of Hindi is not competitive but complementary to the growth of Nepal's national language Nepali and such other languages of the Terai as Maithili, Bhojpuri and Awadhi.

It is in the interest of all the Nepalese that Hindi is officially re-accepted as a medium of instruction in the educational institutions, especially in the Terai region. Since the literature for teaching in Maithili, Bhojpuri and Awadhi is lacking now, the medium of instruction and teaching materials should be Hindi from the primary to the university level education. Such a measure would also help Nepali-speaking undergraduate and graduate students who have to take recourse to Hindi-medium reading materials in view of their deficiency in English and dearth of reading materials in the Nepali medium.

Except in Maithili, there is a lack of adequate literature in other native languages of the Madheshi community. Maithili is the only language which does have a long rich tradition of written literature. However, it is a long way for Awadhi, Bhojpuri and other Terai languages before they can be used as a medium of instruction at school-level education. This gap in the demand and supply of literature could be filled by the Madheshi intellectuals. The Non-Governmental Organizations (NGOs) and charitable institutions could also support this cause. Additionally, the state should also come forward to help prepare textbooks at least for primary level education in such native languages, as Hindi, Maithili, Bhojpuri and Awadhi.

Recently, the Indian government has incorporated Nepali, as the national language of Nepal, in the eighth schedule of its constitution despite the fact that the share of the Nepali-speaking population in the total population of India is very marginal. Like the Nepali language, Urdu, the national language of Pakistan, has already been accepted in the eighth schedule of the Indian Constitution. Incorporation of Nepali in the eighth schedule of the Indian Constitution has, in fact, given an opportunity to the Nepali-speaking population in India to compete in various public service examinations as they might write in Nepali as well.

If India can accept the national languages of foreign countries, like Pakistan and Nepal, in its constitution, there is no reason why the state should feel unwilling to accept Hindi, the national language of India, as one of the mediums of instructions in academic institutions and also in the public service commission examinations. There is also no reason why this language should not receive due coverage in the electronic and print media. This is more so warranted as Hindi is spoken by a majority of the people in the Terai as well as in hills as first, second and third languages; and each year over 30 percent of the Nepalese students receive education in the Indian educational institutions in Hindi.

Notes

1. Mishra, Krishna Chandra, Nepal Ki Bhasa Samasya Samadhan Ya Takarao? Kya Chahate Hain Aap?, (Hindi), Krishna Chandra Mishra, 1990, no page.
2. Thakur, Raghunath, *Partantra Madhesh Aur Uski Sanskriti,* Morang, 1959, pp. 21-24.
3. Ibid.
4. Mishra, No. 1.
5. Gaige, Frederich H., *Regionalism and National Unity in Nepal,* Vikas Publishing House Pvt. Ltd., Delhi, 1975, p. 108.
6. Ibid., p. 109.
7. Ibid., pp. 116-17.
8. *Gorkhapatra,* June 7, 1992.
9. Gaige, No. 5.
10. Ibid., p. 111.

11. Ibid.
12. Devkota, Grishma Bahadur, Nepalko Rajnitik Darpan, Dhruba Bahadur Devkota, Kathmandu, 1979, p. 546.
13. Ibid.
14. Ibid.
15. Ibid., p.111.
16. Ibid, pp. 545-46.
17. Ibid., p. 112.
18. Mishra, No 1.
19. Sadbhavana Sandesh, October 15, 1991, p.3.
20. Ibid.
21. Ibid.
22. Ibid.
23. *The Rising Nepal*, July 8, 1992, p. 1.
24. Ibid.
25. Mishra, No 1.
26. Ibid.
27. Rohra, Satish Kumar and Singh, Surajbhan (ed.), *Hindi Shikshan: Antarrastriya Paripreksha,* (Hindi), Kendriya Hindi Sansthan, Agra,

    1988, p. 138. Also see, Mishra, Kiran, *Nepal Me Hindi Bhasha Avam Sahitya Ki Stithi Ka Parigyan*, (Hindi), Varanasi, 1990, p. 97.
28. Burghart, Richard, "The Formation of the Concept of the Nation-State in Nepal", *Journal of Asian Studies*, Vol. XLIV, No. 1, November 1984, p.121.
29. Gaige, No. 5, p. 119.
30. Thakur, No. 2.
31. Ibid.

32. Videha, May 1, 1992.

33. HMG/N, Ministry of Law, Justice and Parliamentary Affairs, *The Constitution of the Kingdom of Nepal* (1990), Law Books Management Board, Kathmandu, 1992.

34. Das, J.L., "Nepal Adhirajya Ka Sambidhan 2047 Antargat Bhasha Sambandhi Awadharana", Sahitya Loka, 1992, pp. 11-12.

4

MIGRATION AND ITS IMPACT ON THE TERAI

Introduction

An impression is being created by certain quarters that a substantial section of the Madheshi population consists of immigrants from India. But it is far from the reality. Dor Bahadur Bista maintains that the majority of the Madheshi people are indigenous.[1] R.D. Aajad states that the Madheshi people are part and parcel of the Terai land and they did not come from outside.[2] Shankar Lal Kedia presents a glorious picture of the Madheshi community ever since the ancient times.[3] In fact, these people have always been there on this land, though it is a different question that sometimes they were under the rule of their own rulers; at other times under the Mughal emperors; sometimes under the British East India Company; and now under the Nepalese rulers.

The fact that the Madheshi people had their own identity is evidenced by the facts that they sometimes resisted the British East India Company and and also opposed the Gorkha rulers. It is a historical fact that during the war between the British East India Company and Nepal in 1815, they resisted in favour of the British Government. Without a strong base it would not have been possible for those people to do so.

When the British Government began to return certain Terai lands to the Nepalese king in 1816, a year after the Sugauli Treaty, it entered into an agreement with Nepal that the Madheshi people would not be prosecuted on account of having favoured the cause of the British Government during the war between Nepal and British-India in 1815. In Article 7 of the Memorandum for the approval and acceptance of the Rajah of Nepal on December 8, 1816, it is stated, "...the Rajah of Nepal agrees to refrain from prosecuting any inhabitants of the Terai, after its reversion to his rule, on account of having favoured the cause of the British Government during the war and should any of those persons, excepting the cultivators of the soil, be desirous of quitting their estates, and of retiring within the Company's territories, he shall not be liable to hindrance".[4]

Following the conquest of the Terai, land grants were made by the Nepalese rulers to encourage migration in the Terai. Yet people from outside hardly settled there until the middle of the 20th century because of an extremely virulent type of malaria, which the local people called aul. Not even an occasional traveller dared to spend a single night in the Terai, the reason being the risk of exposure to the disease-bearing mosquitoes especially during the "fever season' between April and October. Each year over two million people were attacked by malaria and nearly 10 percent of them died.[5]

The United States Agency for International Development (USAID), the World Health Organization (WHO), and HMG/N were made to combat the malaria through the Nepal Malaria Eradication Organization (NMEO) from 1958. Within a few years of the introduction of NMEO, the horror of the disease reduced considerably. The malaria infection reduced from two million cases a year in the 1950s to less than 2,500 in 1968.[6]

Wider publicity was given to the malaria eradication programme in different hill regions of Nepal to encourage the people to migrate to the Terai. This programme could have encouraged the immigration of people from across the border in India as well from such states, as Bengal, Bihar, and Uttar Pradesh. One of its reasons was that people across the border were perhaps as land hungry as the people in the Nepalese hills. The Treaty of Peace and Friendship concluded between Nepal and India in 1950 also provided the Indian nationals the right of ownership of property and the right to participate in trade and commerce. Article VII of this Treaty states, "The Governments of India and Nepal agree to grant, on a reciprocal basis, to the nationals of one country in the territories of the other the same privileges in the matter of residence, ownership of property, participation in trade and commerce, movement and other privileges of a similar nature".[7]

In order to make the provision of Article VII of the Treaty of Peace and Friendship null and void, the Panchayat Government imposed strict "citizenship" laws. Accordingly, no Indian national could buy land or enter into any economic or commercial activity in Nepal.[8]

Having imposed the citizenship rule strictly, it became easier for the Panchayat Government to restrict the prospective flow of Indian migrants in Nepal; and then to encourage the migration of population from the Nepalese hills to the Terai with an objective of "Nepalization' or what some scholars also call Paharization' of the Madheshi community.

In order to divert the attention of the international community from the state-supported migration of population from the hills to the Terai, false publicity was given that the Terai was having an influx of Indian population. Many Nepalese in the Terai who came through marital relations were also branded as Indian immigrants. Mangal Prasad Gupta, a Congress worker from Western Terai, once raised a question: "On what basis were the residents of Nepal labelled as foreigners since there are many foreigners who have come here through marital relations?[9]

As a matter of fact, there is no such charm of employment in Nepal which will motivate the Indians to rush. Rishikesh Shaha also holds the view that there has been a considerable shift of population from the Nepali hills to the Terai and not so much from India to the Terai.[10] Fateh Singh Tharu, a prominent leader of the Rastriya Prajatantra Party, maintains that even a beggar in India earns more than a beggar in Nepal and, therefore, there is no attraction for the Indians to migrate and settle in this country.

Migration from the Hills to the Terai

In Nepal, it was mainly from the 1950s that the migration of population started from the hills to the Terai. Factors like population pressure, scarcity of arable land, limited food production, underemployment/ unemployment and indebtedness in the hills were some of the push factors responsible for the migration of the population to the Terai. On the other hand, apart from the eradication of malaria, planned resettlement, government incentives and prospect of employment opportunities were some of the positive factors that encouraged migration to the Terai.

Efforts were also made to encourage the migration of population from the hills to the Terai at the institutional level. Rapti Valley Development Plan (RVDP) (1954) was the first such resettlement project introduced in Rapti Valley in Chitwan district of the Terai. At the time when RVDP was introduced there were 36,000 indigenous Tharus in the Valley. But within a few years in 1967, the population of the Valley grew by tenfold.[11] The success of RVDP led HMG/N to increase the number of resettlement projects significantly.

In 1964, the Nepal Resettlement Company (NRC) was established to execute the planned resettlement.

Accordingly, many resettlement projects were set up in different parts of the Terai. The Department of Resettlement of HMG/N distributed land and food grains to the migrants in the resettlement areas. Land was made available to these people free of cost initially and at a nominal price in the later stage. Additionally, education, health and other facilities were also provided.

Those who could not be given land by NRC and/or Department of Resettlement of HMG/N cleared the forest illegally and settled there as squatters. Nearly 77,700 hectares of forest land in the Terai was distributed among migrants and an additional 237,600 hectares of forest land was encroached upon illegally.[12] Thus, the informal encroachment of forests was nearly three times more than the formal clearance of the forest. Subsequently, between 1973 and 1979 the Department of Resettlement distributed 34,771 hectares of land among the migrants.

At present, six resettlement projects are being run; Jhapa Resettlement Project, Sarlahi Resettlement Project, Nawalparasi Resettlement Project, Taratal Resettlement Project, Kailali Resettlement Project, and Kanchanpur Resettlement Project. All these resettlement projects were established by clearing the dense forest land. Apart from the hill migrants, the refugees from Burma, Aasam, and other places were also made to settle there. On the contrary, the landless people in the Terai were rarely given any land in such resettlement projects.

A committee was also formed under the chairmanship of the late Prime Minister Tank Prasad Acharya to recommend the names of the political victims with the view to providing them land in the Terai. Accordingly, many politicians and hill elites in the name of "political victims' were allotted land in Nawalparasi, Sarlahi and other districts by clearing the forest land.

Above all, HMG/N set up "Ban Sudridhikaran Aayojana' (Forest Strengthening Project) at a political level in various districts of the Terai under the chairmanship of a member of the National Panchayat. The members of this Project were given powers and privileges to find out barren and unclaimed land with the purpose of distributing it among the squatters. Until 1990, the Project received thousands of applications from so-called squatters every year and accordingly the land was distributed among them almost free of cost. In the name of squatters, only those cunning applicants who had access to Kathmandu's power circles were given land.

Many unscrupulous elements in the name of squatters encroached and destroyed the forest and declared such land as barren or unclaimed. This had a demonstration effect. Encroachment of the forest land developed as a profession. After establishing claim over the forest land at one place, the encroachers sold it and moved to another district for the same job. This process continued unabated.

At places the land along the banks of the rivers was treated as an unclaimed land. Even the public places of the native villagers were declared as unclaimed land. Such native communities as Rajbanshis/Tharus who tilled land for generations without bothering to register it with the government were evicted from the ownership of land and property. This created a problem of pasture land and environment.

Following the introduction of the Land Reforms Act 1964 in the country, land above the fixed ceiling was acquired by HMG/N. But the local landless Madheshi people were denied their share in this land.

In fact, protecting forest land was hardly any one's business. During the National Referendum in 1980 alone, the forest wood amounting to Rs. 1 billion was destroyed.[13]

In the early 1980s, HMG/N constituted a committee under the chairmanship of Harka Bahadur Gurung to study the internal and international migration of population in Nepal. This committee failed to recommend measures to control migration and reduce the magnitude of environmental degradation. Instead, it recommended to destroy the remaining forest south of the East West Highway and convert it into an agricultural land. It also suggested to encourage further migration of population there.[14] It was equally faulty on the part of this committee to recommend that multi-entry permit/single entry permit system and passport system should be introduced for the Terai community so as to restrict their movement between Nepal and India.[15] The Madheshi intellectuals strongly opposed such ideas and consequently they could not be implemented.[16]

Encroachment of the forest could not be checked even after the restoration of democracy in 1990. It has, rather, increased substantially thereafter. During the National Seminar on "The Terai Community and National Integration in Nepal", Brikhesh Chandra Lal, Mayor of Janakpur Municipality, observed that the migration from the hills to the Terai could not have been so serious in nature had there been horizontal division of the country on the basis of geographical area, like the Himalayan region, the hill region and the Terai region. This was so because the division of the country horizontally could have created an opportunity for the proper development of all the three regions independently. Development, thus, in the Himalayan region or in the hills could have checked the migration of the people from the hills to the Terai.

Seasonal and Permanent Migration from Terai to India

Migration of the population has created imbalances in the Terai. As a result, many of the native people are forced to migrate outside in search of jobs during certain seasons. There are also people who migrate and settle in India permanently.

Till the 1970s, there had been a seasonal migration of population from the adjoining regions of Bengal, Bihar and Uttar Pradesh states of India to the Terai. The Indian labourers helped to cultivate and harvest agricultural crops. But the labourers from across the border stopped coming to Nepal because of the new development opportunities in several parts of India, particularly in the Punjab and Haryana states. Now this process is reversed. It is the Madheshi labourers from almost all the districts of the Terai who now go to the different parts of India, including the Punjab and Haryana states, in certain seasons for employment mainly in the agricultural sector. The wages earned by the Madheshi labourers in India are higher than what they usually get in Nepal.

In addition, many Madheshi people, like the Tharus and Satars, are being forced to migrate to India permanently. The Tharus inhabiting traditionally the forest areas are by and large illiterate and submissive. They easily fall victims to the elite migrants. A great number of these native people are cheated and made virtually paupers. In due course, these landless people are made to serve as Kamaiyas or slaves on their own land. The Kamaiya system has been highly oppressive in nature. In such districts of Far Western Terai, as Banke, Bardia, Kailali and Kanchanpur, the shameful Kamaiya system remained in practice for a long time.

In the past, thousands of Tharus from Dang, Banke, Bardia, Kailali and Kanchanpur were forced to migrate to India as a result of the Kamaiya system. Similarly, there was also a large scale migration of the Tharus from Chitwan district to the regions across the Nepal India border. Before the introduction of Rapti Valley Resettlement Project (RVRP), the entire Chitwan district was full of Tharu population. But now they are virtually reduced to non-entitys in their own land.

Many Satars and other tribal population of Jhapa were also forced to migrate to India. Further work needs to be undertaken to identify how many of these unfortunate native people were forced to quit their villages and migrate to India.

Lakhimpur constituency of Uttar Pradesh state in India is one of the destinations of the Tharu migrants. Likewise, Champaran district in Bihar state has sheltered the Tharus migrated from Chitwan district. The Santhal district in Bihar has become the home of Satar migrants from Jhapa district.

Indira Gandhi, the late Prime Minister of India, is reported to have helped especially the Tharu migrants from Nepal to settle in certain settlements of Uttar Pradesh state in India across the Nepalese border. Education, health and several other facilities are provided to these people. It was gathered that seats have also been reserved for these Tharu migrants in the state medical colleges in Uttar Pradesh.

East West Highway and Migration

During the Rana regime, Padma Road was constructed all along the southern side of the Terai. This fair weather road touches most of the densely populated villages and towns of the Terai. It had potentiality to be developed as a highway; however, it was deliberately ignored. Instead of developing the Padma Road, the present East West Highway which avoids almost all the traditional densely populated areas of the Terai was constructed.

The East-West Highway is responsible for the large scale migration of population from the hills and also for the destruction of thick forest. In addition, its impact on the environment is worst.[17] A day will come when the Nepalese people could analyse the cost-benefit of the Highway and they would be puzzled to know about the harm inflicted by this to the Terai region in particular and the nation as a whole in general.

NRC/Resettlement Department and Migration

Apart from the Highway, the NRC and the Resettlement Department are also responsible for the migration and destruction of forests in the Terai. A government publication shows that 90 percent of the resettlements have been developed by the Resettlement Department in the Terai alone, which used to be thick forest land. By 1927, a little less than half of the Terai land was covered with forests. But by 1977 the percentage of forest land reduced to a fifth of its total area.[18] And between 1977 and 1992, i.e. during 15 years, there is hardly any thick forest left anywhere except in the national parks. It has been accepted in a government publication that the migration of population from the hills to the Terai "encouraged deforestation and encroachment on state lands in the Terai and for the short run at least, has taxed the economic and social service sectors".[19]

Survey Result

The following survey result gives an account of the perception of the Madheshi community about the migration problem in Nepal.

Knowledge About Migration

Table 4.1 presents that as much as 98 percent of the total sample households have knowledge about the migration of the population in the Terai. Only 2 percent of them are ignorant of this problem.

Table 4.1: Knowledge About Migration

Categories	*Number of Households*	*Percentage*
Yes	982	98
No	18	2
Total	1000	100

Source: Field Survey, 1992

Origin of the Migrants

The following table shows that of the total sample households, 93 percent think that those who migrate into the Terai come from the hills. About 6 percent of them have a feeling that the migration is from one district of the Terai to the other. And the rest 1 percent think that the migration is from India to the Terai.

Table 4.2: Concept About the Origin of the Migrants

Origin	*Number of Households*	*Percentage*
Hills to Terai	912	93
Terai to Terai	63	6
India to Terai	7	1
Other Country to Terai	-	-
Total	1000	100

Source: Field Survey, 1992

Period of Migration

Table 4.3 presents the views of the sample households about the period for which the migrants stay in the Terai. About 92 percent of the households have a feeling that the people who migrate to the Terai region settle there permanently; whereas 5 percent think that they stay for a long period of time. Merely 2 percent of the households state that the migrants stay for a short period of time.

Table 4.3: Perception About the Period of Migration

Period of Migration	*Number of Households*	*Percentage*
Short Period	24	2
Long Period	53	5
Permanently	905	92
Total	1000	100

Source: Field Survey, 1992

Note: Migration for the short period means such migration which takes place for a few months only; whereas the migration for the long period means migration for years; and permanent migration denotes migration for all the time.

Land Area Occupied by the Migrants

Table 4.4 indicates the views of the sample households about the nature of land occupied by the migrants. About 40 percent of the sample households have a feeling that the migrants settled in the rural and urban areas; 34 percent think that they settled in the deforested land; and 1 percent think that they settled in the barren/ unclaimed land. However, 25 percent of the households state that the migrants occupied all sorts of land, including rural/urban, forest covered, and barren/unclaimed areas.

Table 4.4: Concept About the Land Area Occupied by Migrants

Nature of Geographical Location	*Number of Households*	*Percentage*
Land in Rural/ Urban Area	397	40
Forest Covered Area	334	34
Barren Land	10	1
All of the above	241	25
Total	1000	100

Source: Field Survey, 1992

Land Distribution in the Resettlement Projects

As much as 83 percent of the sample households hold the view that the Madheshi squatters have not been given land in the resettlement projects; 1 percent believe that they have been given land; and the remining 16 percent have no idea about it (Table 4.5).

Table 4.5: Distribution of Land Among the Mdheshi Squatters in the Resettlement Projects

Responses	*Number of Households*	*Percentage*
Yes	15	1
No	827	83
Don't Know	158	16
Total	1000	100

Source: Field Survey, 1992

Attitude Towards the Migrants

Table 4.6 indicates that as much as 68 percent of the households are neutral about the migrants; 16 percent regard them as friends; and the remaining 16 percent considar them as rivals. The reaction, thus, of the households towards the migrants appear to be mixed.

Table 4.6: Attitude Towards the Migrants

Categories	*Number of Households*	*Percentage*
As Friends	157	16
As Rivals	154	16
Neutral	671	68
Total	1000	100

Source: Field Survey, 1992

Impact of Migration

It was reported by certain households that in the past the migration in the Terai helped reduce cultural barriers and promote the level of understanding between the Madheshi and the hill community. However, it was also added that the migrants tilled unclaimed and fallow land and this created problems of pasture land. Besides, the migration also caused the shortage of cultivable land. It was also reported that one of the impacts of the migration is the shortage of herbs, fuelwood and timber as there is no more forest to meet their supply. This affected the source of income of those local people who by tradition sold such forest products in the market. It has also added to their unemployment problem.

There was a feeling that the migration in the Terai has been exerting pressure on the local resources to such an extent that many of the Madheshi people are being forced to migrate to different states of India.

According to Table 4.7, 48 percent of the total sample households share the view that the migration of the population from the hills to the Terai adversely affects the socio-economic and environmental conditions in the Terai. Such households which feel that the migration does not have any adverse impact form 16 percent of the sample households. However, those who are ignorant about the impact of migration constitute 36 percent of the households.

Table 4.7: Opinion About the Socio-Economic and Environmental Impact of Migration

Categories	*Number of Households*	*Percentage*
Adverse Impact	467	48
No Adverse Impact	160	16
Don't Know	355	36
Total	1000	100

Source: Field Survey, 1992

Conclusion

The migration of population from the hills to the Terai has raised regional, ethnic and political issues. Tensions prevail between local Terai people and migrants, though on a limited scale now. There have also been occasions when the Madheshi people protested against the migration and also the state policies which support this trend. One of the government publications states, "The protest against the "Gurung Report" by a substantial section of the eastern Terai population was, principally, a protest against the in-migration of the Pahadis and the state policies which encourage such in-migration.[20]

In addition to the Terai, the hill economy is affected on account of migration. It has created labour shortage in the hills. There is a mismanagement of land and production specially among those migrants who retain agricultural land in the hills. Besides, migration has been affecting the development process in the hills and has, thus, widened the disparity in the resource base and developmental infrastructure between these regions [Terai and hills].[21]

Because of the over-strain on the use of natural resources, such as forest, agricultural land, environment, and rivers, there has been shortage of rainfall, decline in the water table in the rivers and soil, irregular monsoon, and desertification in several parts of the Terai. It cannot be denied that these problems are partly due to migration.

It is stated in one of the World Bank's publications, "...the Terai is already saturated".[22] Under such a situation, the migration issue in Nepal will create further tensions and thus affect the process of national integration. Such tensions will grow increasingly if the rate of agricultural, industrial, service and urban sectors is slow.[23] Aparna Tripathi and K.S. Nagar, therefore, conclude, "If the Nepal Government sticks to migration and other such negative steps and policies, the Terai problem is likely to remain unsolved".[24]

Considering some of these developments, it is essential to stop the existing trend of converting the state land under the forest into private land in the name of developing resettlements for the squatters. Effective protection should be given to the remaining forests south and north of the East West Highway. All the forest land in the Terai should be given the status of national park and necessary protection should be given to the plants and wild animals living there. The remaining Terai forest could be protected if it is given the same protection as Shukla Fanta of Kanchanpur or Bardia National Parks of Bardia. Experience of India could also be shared in regard to protecting forests. India has well managed and protected its Dudhwa National Park across the Nepalese border in Far Western Nepal.

Finally, a long-term plan should be envisaged to discourage further migration of population from the hills to the Terai. Wherever possible the Madheshi squatters and landless people should also be accommodated in the existing resettlements. This is not only justified on moral grounds but also on the ground of maintaining national unity.

Notes

1. Bista, Dor Bahadur, *Fatalism and Development: Nepal's Struggle for Modernization,* Orient Longman Limited, Hyderabad, 1991, p. 49.
2. Aajad, R.D., *Terai Jal Rahi Hai,* (Hindi), (no date, no place), p. 63.
3. Kedia, Shankar Lal, *Madheshiya Samaj Aur Uski Utpatti,* (Hindi), Nepal Terai Vidyarthi Bhasa Abam Sanskriti Samanwya Samiti, Kathmandu, 1991, pp. 1-23.
4. Aitchison, C.U. (Comp.), *A Collection of Treaties, Engagements and Sanads Relating to India and Neighbouring Countries,* Superintendent Government Printing, Calcutta, 1909, p. 114.
5. Moran, Kerry, *Partnership for Development: forty Years of American Assistance,* US AID, 1991, p. 17.
6. Ibid.
7. Treaty of Peace and Friendship, Kathmandu, July 31,1950.
8. Baral, Lok Raj, *Regional Migrations, Ethnicity and Security: The South Asian Case,* Sterling Publishers Private Limited, New Delhi, 1990, p. 3.
9. HMG/N, *National Commission on Population, Proceedings of the National Seminar on Population and Environment,* Kathmandu, July 3-4, 1989, p. 42.
10. Shaha, Rishikesh, "Guidelines from Experiences" *in Future of South Asia,* (ed. Chopra, Pran and et al), Macmillan India Limited, Delhi, 1986, p. 159.

11. Moran, no. 5.
12. HMG/N, National Commission on Population, *Inter-Regional Migration in Nepal: Problem and Prospects,* Kathmandu, 1984, pp.83.
13. Pant, Shastra Dutta, *Vyabasthit Vasti Ra Gaun Vikas,* (Nepali), South Asian research Centre, Kathmandu, 1992.
14. National Commission on Population, *Nepalma Aantarik Tatha Antarrastriya Basai-Sarai,* (Nepali), Kathmandu, 1983, pp. 498-99.
15. Ibid., pp. 482.
16. Jha, Hari Bansh, "Gurung Report: A Pandora's Box", *Media Nepal,* Vol. 1, No. 1., Kathmandu, 2041, pp. 25-32.
17. Shrestha, Bijaya Lal, "East to West, A Highway to the Future", Himal, September/October, 1990, p.13.
18. HMG/N, no. 8, p. 84.
19. HMG/N, National Commission on Population, *Population and Development in Nepal,* Kathmandu, 1988, p. 107.
20. Ibid.
21. Ibid.
22. Document of the World Bank, *Nepal Relieving Poverty in a Resource-Scarce Economy,* Volume I, 1990, p. 30.
23. HMG/N, No. 19.
24. Tripathi, Aparna and Nagar, K.S., "Nepal's Ethnic Divide and India", paper presented at an International Seminar on "Indo-Nepalese Relations; Anthroponomical and Geo-Economic Linkages", organized by Centre for the Study of Nepal, Banaras Hindu University, Varanasi, March 24-26, 1990, p. 9.

5

ECONOMY OF THE TERAI

Introduction

The share of the Terai in Nepal's total land area is merely 17 percent. However, it contains over 50 percent of the total population of the country. In the GDP, the share of this region is about 63 percent. Similarly, its contribution to the total national agricultural product is nearly 55 percent.[1]

The main sources of income for the Terai people include agricultural farming, livestock, horticulture, fishery, service, etc. Cows, buffalos, goats and other domestic animals help them earn their income. Besides, they also earn by making handicraft items, such as baskets, artistic and modern furniture, ornaments of silver and gold, etc.

It is mainly at the local *haat bazaars* (small market-places) that most of the agricultural, industrial and handicraft items are sold. Such *haat bazaars* play a crucial role in the economy of the Terai people. But the lack of adequate infrastructural facilities, such as roads and bridges, pose a great problem in the promotion of the *haat bazaars*.

Agriculture

The Terai, possessing 70 percent of the total cultivated

land in the country,[2] is called the'grain basket' of Nepal. Normally, part of the grain produced in this region is either supplied to the food deficit hills of Nepal or outside. But during the draught there is deficit of food grains in this region. Irrigated land allows three or even four harvests a year. But the larger portions of the cultivable land is unirrigated. If the monsoon is not favourable, it creates problems. But life becomes easier if the monsoon is adequate. A good monsoon is the symbol of prosperity as it helps to grow paddy, the major food grain of the Terai.

The cultivable land turns green from July to February when paddy is grown. Apart from paddy, wheat, sugarcane, lentils, maize, cotton and all such fruits and vegetables which could be grown in a climate tempered by the adjacent Himalayas are produced.

It was under the Land Act 1964 that a ceiling on land was introduced in Nepal. Accordingly, no individual in the Terai could possess more than 17.175 hectares of land for farming; and 2.061 hectares for housing. Between 1964 and 1992, there has been further division in the cultivated land as a result of an increase in the number of population.

Due to the sub-division of land holding, the average land holding size is 1.89 hectares. This is extremely small. According to the Agricultural Statistics of Nepal (1990), the population density per hectare of cultivable land in the Terai is 3.6.[3]

Industry

The Terai accounts for over 70 percent of the total industrial production in Nepal. The share of the small industries of this region in the total small industries of the country is 72 percent. Most of the industries in this region process agricultural products, like rice. Oil mills are found in rural as well as urban areas. These processing units are being run in the private sector on a small scale.

Most of the industries established in the Terai are located in the rural areas creating pollution of air and water. This becomes perceptible if an account is taken of the growth of industries between Biratnagar and Itahari, Janakpur and Dhalkewar, Birgunj and Pathalahiya, and Bhairahawa and Butwal.

Until recently, HMG/N used to earn a lot of money by exporting the timber of the Terai forest to India. Even now when the forest resources are being largely depleted, the smuggling of timber from Nepal to India is continuing. The depletion of the forest resources by elements close to the ruling circles have caused concern for the environmentalists. The establishment of the giant saw mills and brick factories are also responsible for depleting the green and immature trees in the Terai.

Tourism

The countryside of the Terai with green, red or yellow foliage and groves, and orchards of mangoes and lychees are attractive. Bamboo and jackfruit trees are also enjoyable. The vegetation attracts bees to create hives. The ponds are in abundance. They are used for irrigation as well as for growing fish. One can relax by bathing in the ponds.

Additionally, the presence of Janakpur and Lumbini in the Terai region is also a source of attraction to pilgrims, especially the Hindus and Buddhists. Janakpur happens to be the birth place of Goddess Sita, wife of Lord Ramchandra. Similarly, Lumbini is the birth place of Lord Buddha.

In the past, the government helped to complete a master plan of Lumbini. In Janakpur, too, there is a plan to constracta larger circular road. But this is not adequate. The master plan of Janakpur and Lumbini should be made in such a way that they should get linked to the different religious centres of India. For example, Janakpur could be linked to Dhanusha, Girija Asthan, Sitamadhi and other such places of religious importance. Similarly,

Lumbini could be linked to Sarnath, Gaya, Kushinagar and other historical places in India. A joint effort on the part of HMG/N and the Government of India is needed to give concrete shape to this idea.

Until some years ago, such melas, as Ramnavmi and Bibahapanchami used to be organized with great enthusiasm at Janakpur. A large number of businessmen from different parts of Nepal and India used to sell various items on such occasions. Importance of these melas declined ever since the custom authorities started imposing custom duties on such items.

Whatever remaining thick forest that is left in the Terai could also attract foreign tourists. Chitwan National Park has attracted many tourists; it is due to the establishment of the resort centres and recreational facilities there. Resort centres and recreational facilities, if developed in other national parks, such as Bardia National Park, Shukla Fanta National Park and the other forest areas, could also attract foreign tourists.

Concerns of the Terai

The role of the Terai in the development of the country is not properly recognized. The policy makers and development agencies have neglected many of its concerns. During the Panchayat regime, it was not allowed to set up industries in the Terai up to 8 kms. of the Indian border.[4]

Abundance in the Terai is for the few. Many people live in acute misery and poverty and they are not even in a position to make a living. Every year the people, especially of the labour class, are forced to leave their home in search of food and work. They go to such far-off places, as Delhi, Bengal, Bihar, Aassam, Uttar Pradesh, Punjab and Haryana states of India; and work mainly in the agricultural fields. Some of these people also reach Kathmandu and engage themselves in petty businesses like selling vegetables and fruits. But unfortunately these people are branded in Kathmandu as Indian.

In one study conducted at Tribhuvan University, it was found, "the percentage of the households heads reporting worsened life conditions is higher in the Terai than in the hills... a higher percentage of hill households heads are more positive and optimistic about the future than Terai households heads".[5]

Survey Result

During the survey, information was collected from the sample households about their occupation, irrigation facilities, land holding size, land use pattern, income and expenditure. Some of these aspects have been analysed below:

Occupation

Table 5.1 indicates that as much as 81 percent of the total sample households depend on agriculture for their livelihood followed by service (10 percent), and industry and trade (9 percent).

Table 5.1: Occupation

Categories	*Number of Households*	*Percentage*
Agriculture	812	81
Industry & Trade	90	9
Service	98	10
Total	1000	100

Source: Field Survey, 1992

Irrigation

Table 5.2 shows that of the total cultivated land of the sample households, 82 percent land is unirrigated. Irrigated land accounts for only 18 percent of the total cultivated land.

Table 5.2: Irrigation of Cultivated Land

Type of Land	*Percentage*
Irrigated	18
Unirrigated	82
Total	100

Source: Field Survey, 1992

Land Holding Size

Table 5.3 indicates that one-third (33 percent) of the total sample households are landless. Households having land upto 0.687 hectares form 32 percent followed by those who hold land between 0.687 and 3.435 hectares (28 percent), between 3.435 and 6.870 hectares (5 percent) and above 6.870 hectares (2 percent). The average land holding size of the households is 1.89 hectares.

Landlessness is one of the major problems in the Terai. Besides, small land holding size is also a problem. The share of the households possessing 6.870 hectares of land *or* above is marginal.

Table 5.3: Land Holding Size (Hectares)

Land Holding Size	*Number of Households*	*Percentage*
Landless -	329	33
Upto - 0.687	318	32
0.687 - 3.435	282	28
3.435 - 6.870	55	5
Above 6.870	16	2
Total	1000	100

Source: Field Survey, 1992.

Land Use Pattern

Table 5.4 shows that in the sample survey area 89 percent of the cultivated land is used for cereal crop production. Next to it, vegetables are grown on 8 percent of the land and fruit on 3 percent of land.

In the Terai, the cost of cultivation has been growing. This is due to an increase in labour cost as well as price of different inputs, such as seeds, fertilizers, pesticides, etc. Use of pesticides and fertilizers is irregular and haphazard. Original fertility of the soil has been declining.

Table 5.4: Land Use Pattern (Hectares)

Crops Grown	*Cultivated Land*	*Percentage*
Cereal Crops	1687	89
Fruit	56	3
Vegetable	155	8
Total	1898	100

Source: Field Survey, 1992

Income and Income Inequality

Table 5.5 indicates that 18 percent of the total sample households earn upto Rs. 10,000 a year and 11 percent over Rs. 40,000. Moreover, 43 percent of them earn between Rs. 10,000 and Rs. 20,000, and 28 percent between Rs. 20,000 and Rs. 40,000.

The table shows that the share of the bottom 18 percent of the households in the total gross income of the sample households is merely 6 percent while the same of the top 11 percent of the households is as high as 32 percent. This shows that there is a great disparity in the distribution of income among the different sections of the Madheshi community.

According to the sample data, the per capita income of the Madheshi people is Rs. 3,969, which if compared to the per capita GDP of Nepal of Rs. 5,704 at the current price, is lower by 30 percent.[6]

Per capita income of the Madheshi people is low due to the fact that one-third of them are landless and agriculture farming does not give them sufficient returns. Farming practices to a great extent are primitive. Lack of adequate transportation and storage facilities create problems in transporting agricultural products to the market. Alternative sources of income from industry, business and service sectors are limited.

Table 5.5: Annual Income

Income Size (Rs)	*Number of Sample Households*	*Percentage*	*Gross Income (Rs)*	*Percentage*
Upto - 10000	182	18	1540250	6
10000 - 20000	431	43	6314280	27
20000 - 40000	277	28	8314800	35
Above 40000	110	11	7643300	32
Total	1000	100	23812630	100

Source: Field Survey, 1992

Population Below Poverty Line

In Table 5.6, three estimates of poverty are given - the first estimate is of NPC, the second is based on the international definition of absolute poverty of US $ 150, and the third is of Lipton which is equally recognized.

On the basis of the NPC estimate, the population below the poverty line is found to be 28 percent in the Terai, 52 percent in the hills and 40 percent in Nepal. However, this estimate is said to be too conservative.

On the basis of the internationally accepted definition of income equivalent to US $ 150 per capita per annum, 68 percent of the total population in the Terai, 75 percent in the hills and 71 percent in Nepal are below the poverty line.

According to Lipton's estimate of incidence of poverty, 68 percent of the total population in the Terai are below the poverty line whereas the corresponding figures for the hills and Nepal are 64 percent and 66 percent, respectively.

The findings of the study are similar to Lipton's estimate in the sense that both these sources reveal that the incidence of poverty is more serious in the Terai than in the hills.

Table 5.6: Incidence of Poverty Under Different Poverty Lines (Percentage of Population Below Poverty Line)

Poverty	*Terai*			*Hills*			*Nepal*		
Line	*Rural*	*Urban*	*Total*	*Rural*	*Urban*	*Total*	*Rural*	*Urban*	*Total*
NPC	29%	17%	28%	55%	13%	52%	42%	15%	40%
US$150	69%	51%	68%	78%	32%	75%	74%	42%	71%
Lipton	70%	50%	68%	68%	52%	64%	68%	51%	66%

Source: Nepal Poverty and Income 5.6.7 Sources of Income

An analysis of Table 5.7 shows that the sample households earn substantial portions of their income from agriculture (59 percent) followed by service (23 percent), and industry and trade (18 percent).

Table 5.7: Sources of Income

Sources of Income	*Gross Income*	*Percentage*
Agriculture	14034330	59
Industry & Trade	4220900	18
Service	5557400	23
Total	23812630	100

Source: Field Survey, 1992

Note : * Agriculture includes livestock, poultry, fishing, etc.

** Industry includes all sorts of industries i.e.cottage, medium and large.

Expenditure Pattern

Table 5.8 shows that the sample households earning an annual income upto Rs. 20,000 have a deficit budget whereas those earning an income above this amount have a surplus budget. The per household deficit for those earning an income upto Rs. 10,000 is Rs. 1,092 and for those earning an income between Rs. 10,000 and Rs. 20,000 is Rs. 565.

The following table shows that with an increase in the level of income, the savings increase. Households earning an income between Rs. 20,000 and Rs. 40,000 have a surplus of Rs. 1,175. Similarly, households earning an income over Rs. 40,000 have a surplus of Rs. 13,268.

It was reported by the sample households that the deficit in budget is met by borrowing loans. The private moneylenders still play an important role in the financial market. As much as 70 percent of the total loan is taken from the private money lenders and the remaining 30 percent from the banking sector.

A majority of the households receive loans for meeting their domestic expenditure, like marriages, death rituals, feasts, etc. The share of the loan on such farming activities, as seeds, fertilizers and farm equipment as well as on trade and industry is quite low. The position of loan recovery is also poor.

Table 5.8: Annual Expenditure

Income Size (Rs.)	*No. of Sample HH*	*%*	*Gross Income (Rs.)*	*Gross Expenditure (Rs)*	*Surplus - Deficit (Rs)*	*Per HH Surplus/ Deficit*
Upto-10000	182	18	1540250	1739082	- 198832	- 1092
10000-20000	431	43	6314280	6557652	- 243372	- 565
20000-40000	277	28	8314800	7989395	325405	1175
Above 40000	110	11	7643300	6183800	1459500	13268
Total	1000	100	23812630	22469929	1342701	—

Source: Field Survey, 1992

Sources of Expenditure

Table 5.9 shows that of the total expenditure of the sample households, 56 percent is spent on food items and the remaining 44 percent on non-food items, which is due to the poor economic base of the households.

Table 5.9: Sources of Annual Expenditure

Categories	*Expenditure (Rs)*	*Percentage*
Food Items	12603450	56
Non-food Items	9866479	44
Total	22469929	100

Source: Field Survey, 1992

Women's Self-Dependence

In the sample survey area, as much as 74 percent of the household heads reported that they wish the women to become self-dependent. Such households that wanted women to remain confined to the corridors of their home and live a traditional life constituted only 26 percent.

Table 5.10 shows the perception of those sample households who are in favour of making women self-dependent. Half of such households (50 percent) have a feeling that the women could be self-dependent if they are engaged in cottage industries; 38 percent think that they could be self-dependent if they are engaged in livestock farming; 9 percent state that they could be self-dependent if they are engaged in poultry and fisheries; and the remaining 2 percent reveal that they could be self-dependent if they are engaged in activities like making dry fruits/vegetables and pickles.

There is lack of vision among the interviewed households that the women could also be made self-dependent by employing them in government service, industries, and other organized sectors.

Table 5.10: Perception About Making Women Self-dependent

Areas of Activities	*Number of Households*	*Percentage*
Cottage Industry	423	50
Livestock Farming	320	38
Poultry/Fishery	73	9
Dry Fruits/Vegetables/ Pickles, etc	15	2
Others*	9	1
Total	840	100

Source: Field Survey, 1992

* *Others include jobs in government, industry, service and other organized sectors.*

Conclusion

It is a paradox that despite the Terai region being rich in resources, the Madheshi community is poor. Therefore, sizeable portions of the revenue generated in the Terai should be spent on such development activities which aim at improving the economic condition of the sons of the soil.

All possibilities should be explored to develop the tourism industry in the Terai. For this, it is essential to make master plans with a view to linking Janakpur and Lumbini with other religious centres of Nepal and India. Besides, custom duty should be waived on such items between Nepal and India which aim at reaching the religious melas, such as Ramnavmi and Bibahapanchami.

Resort centres should be established at appropriate locations in the Terai, such as in the forest areas of Bardia National Park, Shukla Fanta National Park, Koshi Tappu, etc. Studies and researches could also be encouraged to discover new areas having the potentiality to attract tourists. Nepal's tourism department as well as diplomatic missions in different countries could also give due attention to the people and places in the Terai having importance from the point of view of tourist attraction.

Development of the agricultural sector is a pre-requisite to increasing food production, raising the supply of raw materials and encouraging savings and investment. Hence, it is essential to increase investment in agricultural sector. Agricultural education, research and training could be launched not in isolation but in an integrated way to improve the agricultural sector.

Efforts should be directed towards the consolidation of land holding in the agricultural sector so as to make it modern. Additionally, crop diversification might be encouraged. Such crops which give maximum returns should be given priority over the traditional ones. In this regard, multiple cropping system could be encouraged.

The cultivation of betel, nut, pepper, coconuts, bananas and pineapples should be introduced in various parts of the Terai as they give higher returns. Also, in view of the climatic advantage for the introduction of sericulture, its farming should be further encouraged.

Demonstrative research should be conducted at the academic and non-academic levels about the ways and means of reducing the cost of production in the agricultural sector. Awareness would have to be raised among the farmers against the haphazard use of chemical fertilizers and pesticides which not only spoil the original productivity of land but also affect the health of the consumers.

Prospect of the growth of livestock farming is high in the Terai. Therefore, the concerned units should extend all possible support to white revolution in this region.

As in the Punjab state of India, green revolution could also be introduced in the Terai region of Nepal. Thousands of Madheshi labourers working in the Punjab have returned with adequate expertise and they could help translate the idea of the green revolution into action.

Special programmes could be launched to provide employment opportunities to women. Programmes such as Production Credit for Rural Women (PCRW) of the Ministry of Local Development could be made effective in the Terai so that more and more women could benefit from different income-generating activities.

Efforts should be directed by the concerned units to ensure that the items that the women produce are easily sold in the market. In this context, cooperatives could be developed to remove marketing bottlenecks for the items to be produced by women.

Special community-based intensive programmes could be launched in different districts of the Terai to address the problems of the destitutes and population below the poverty line. In this regard, training could be provided to the people taking into consideration their hereditary skills. For example, the blacksmiths could be trained in making tools, the *chamars* in skin-related items, and the *doms* in bamboo-related items.

The education system should be restructured in such a way that skill formation and vocational training should be made integral components of the curricula.

An awareness needs to be created among the Madheshi people to control unproductive expenditure on marriage ceremonies, feasts, death rituals, etc. This will not only help them get rid of the problem of indebtedness but will also contribute to their prosperity. Local government institutions, social workers, religious leaders and the NGOs could play an important role in bringing an attitudinal change among the people in this direction.

Utmost priority should be accorded to the development of infrastructural facilities like irrigation, roads and bridges in the Terai.

It is also necessary to prepare profiles of each and every village and district in the Terai so that common programmes and plans are launched in marketing, research, transport and communication sectors for achieving balanced development of the Terai.

Finally, the duty-free border trade between Nepal and India could prove effective to improve the economic condition of the Madheshi community. Border trade among the people living within the distance of 30 kms. of the Nepal-China (Tibet) border is allowed. If HMG/N and the government of China could provide this facility to the people living along the Nepal-China border, there is no reason why such a facility could not be provided by HMG/N and the Indian government to the people living along the Nepal-India border. If this facility is made available, the entire Terai could be industrialized and the economic condition of the people would be substantially improved because the local people would get an opportunity to benefit from the difference in price of goods between the two countries.

Presently, it is the smugglers and carriers who benefit from the difference in price of goods between Nepal and India. But when the duty-free border trade is legalized, the poor people all along the border in Nepal and India will benefit.

It is, therefore, desirable that HMG/N and the Government of India should enter into a agreement to allow the people living upto a certain distance of the Nepal-India border in both the countries to have border trade. The modus operandi of such trade could be decided by the concerned authorities of the two countries.

Notes

1. *Himal*, September/October 1990, p. 8.
2. Blakie, Piers, Cameron, John and Seddon, David, *Nepal in Crisis: Growth and Stagnation at the Periphery,* Oxford University Press, Delhi, 1980, p. 10.
3. HMG/N, Ministry of Agriculture, Department of Food and Agricultural Marketing Services, *Agricultural Statistics of Nepal 1990,* Lalitpur, 1990, p. 246.
4. Shastri, Sundar Jha, *Ucchastariya Jansankhya Paramarshadatri Samiti Sanga Aek Nimnstariya Byakti Ko Anurodh,* (Nepali), Sundar Jha Shastri, Janakpur Dham, 1985, p. 2.
5. Himal, No. 1.
6. HMG/N, Ministry of Finance, *Economic Survey 1991-92, (Nepali),* Kathmandu, 1992, p. 16.

6

ISSUES IN NATIONAL INTEGRATION

Background

It was partly during the Treaty of Sugauli in 1816 and partly later that the Terai region was handed over by the British East India Company to Nepal.[1] As per this treaty, India was expected to safeguard the interests of the Terai community (Appendix V). However, this commitment remained far from being fulfilled. Ever since the Treaty was concluded between the two countries, the Madheshi people have been facing an identity problem.[2]

The Indian attitude towards the Madheshi people is also a problem in maintaining a separate identity. The Indians are yet to develop knowledge of ethnography of Nepal. In the border areas in India, these people are looked upon, as kith and kin of Bihar and Uttar Pradesh caste groups. In Delhi and other remote parts of India, they are looked upon, as Indian Hindi speakers settled in Nepal. On the other hand, certain sections of the Nepalese population brand the Madheshi people as outsiders.

In Nepal, efforts have been made by the ruling elites to see that the Terai should serve merely economic interests of Kathmandu-based aristocracy without having due participation in national polity. This is because "...the ruling elites-both the Shahs and Ranas-believed that the Terai's development was not in their long-term interest."[3] Rishikesh Shaha maintains, "The Terai people have genuine grievances in so far as they are not adequately represented in the power structure of Nepal, be it in the army, the administration, the national legislature or the cabinet".[4]

Representation

It will be worthwhile to examine the level of representation of Madheshi community in the civil service, army, political parties, parliament and council of ministers for assessing their contribution to nation building. The level of representation of this community in all such fields is discussed below:

Representation in Civil Service and T.U.

Table 6.1 shows the level of representation of the Madheshis in the civil service and in Tribhuvan University (TU). In the civil service, the share of these people at the level of section officer is merely 5 percent. At the level of deputy secretary and secretary, their share is 8 percent and 9 percent, respectively.

As in the civil service, the representation of Madheshis people in TU is also inadequate. The following table shows that the share of these people in the total posts in TU is 15 percent only.

Table 6.1: Representation of Madheshis People in Civil Service and TU

Categories of Posts	*Percent of Madheshi People*	*Percent of Hill People*	*Total*
Section Officer (1989)	5	95	100
Deputy Secretary (1989)	8	92	100
Secretary (1989)	9	91	100
TU (All Posts 1990)	15	85	100

Source: Nepal: Ethnicity in Democracy (Paper)

Tickets Offered by Political Parties to Madheshi Candidates in the General Election (1991)

Table 6.2 shows that NSP is the only political party which distributed the maximum number of tickets to Madheshi candidates during the election of representatives to the House of Representatives. This party allotted 93 percent of its total 75 tickets to Madheshi candidates. However, NC, which claims to be the champion of democracy, could allot merely 19 percent of its total tickcts to Madheshi candidates. The performance of CPN (UML) was not even on par with NC as it allotted merely 16 percent of its total tickets to Madheshi candidates.

Table 6.2: Tickets Offered to Madheshi Candidates by Important Political Parties During the General Election (1991)

Political Parties	*Number of Candidate Madheshi*	*%*	*Number of Candidate*	*Hill %*	*Total*	*%*
NC	38	19	166	81	204	100
CPN (UML)	28	16	149	84	177	100
NSP	70	93	5	7	75	100

Source: Nepal: Ethnicity in Democracy (Paper)

Table 6.3 further shows the place given to Madheshi candidates by eight sample political parties during the election of the representatives to the House of Representatives (1991). Of the total 967 candidates of these political parties, the share of Madheshi candidates was restricted to 27 percent only.

Table 6.3: Madheshi Candidates of Eight Sample Political Parties

Ethnic Candidates	*Number*	*Percentage*
Madheshi	263	27
Hill	704	72
Total	967	100

Source: Himal, May-June, 1992.

Representation of Madheshis in Central Committees of Political Parties

Table 6.4 shows the representation of the Madheshi community in central/working committee of four main political parties in Nepal. For obvious reasons there is total representation of the Madheshi community in the central committee of NSP. But in NC, merely 2 (7 percent) of the 27 members of the working committee are Madheshis. In the Rastriya Prajatantra Party (RPP), 2 (10 percent) of the 20 members of the central committee are Madheshis. And in the central committee of CPN (UML), 3 (8 percent) of the 37 members are Madheshis. Thus, except NSP, the Madheshi community appears to be inadequately represented in all the political parties at the level of the central committee.

Table 6.4: Representation of the Madheshi Community at the Level of Central Committees of Political Parties

Political Parties	*Numbe of Madheshis*	*Total Percentage Leaders at the Level*	*Numbers of Seats of Central Committee*
NC	2	27	7
CPN (UML)	3	37	8
RSP	2	20	10
NSP	35	35	100

Source: Field Survey, 1992.

Madheshi MPs in Political Parties

Table 6.5 presents that of the total MPs of NC in the House of Representatives, the share of Madheshi MPs is 22 percent. Similarly, of the total MPs of CPN (UML) the share of Madheshi MPs is 9 percent. NSP is the only political party which has all its MPs from Madheshi community.

Table 6.5: Madheshi MPs in Political Parties

Political Parties	*Number of Madheshis*	*%*	*Number of Hill MPs*	*%*	*Total MPs*	*%*
NC	24	22	86	78	110	100
CPN (UML)	6	9	62	91	68	100
NSP	6	100	-	-	6	100

Source: Nepal: Ethnicity in Democracy (Paper)

Madheshi MPs in Parliament

Table 6.6 shows the representation of Madheshi MPs in parliament in 1959, 1978, 1981 and 1991 elections. In 1959, the Madheshi MPs in parliament accounted for 22 percent which fell to an all time low to 15 percent in 1978. But the share of this ethnic community increased to 20 percent in 1981. In the present House of Representatives, the share of MPs from this community accounts for 21 percent. Representation of MPs from this community in the National Assembly is 15 percent of the total MPs (60).

Table 6.6: Madheshi MPs in Parliament

MPs from Ethnic Communities	*1959*	*1978*	*1981*	*1991 House of Represe-ntatives*	*1991 National Assembly*	*Both*
Madheshis	22	15	20	21	15	20
Hill	78	85	80	79	85	80
Percent	100	100	100	100	100	100
Total No of Seals	109	129	112	205	60	265

Source: Himal. May/June 1992

Representation in the Council of Ministers

Table 6.7 shows that the share of Madheshi ministers in the council of ministers during the Panchayat regime between 1960 and 1989 was 16 percent. The situation does not seem to have improved much even after the restoration of democracy in 1990. Now the share of the Madheshi ministers in the council of ministers headed by Prime Minister G.P. Koirala accounts for 17 percent only.

Table 6.7: Representation of the Madheshi Community in the Council of Ministers

Categories	*Number of Madheshi Ministers*	*%*	*Number of Hill Ministers*	*%*	*Total*	*%*
Ministers (1960-1989)	35	16	181	84	216	100
Ministers (1992-93)	4	17	20	83	24	100

Source: Nepal: Ethnicity in Democracy (Paper)

Distribution of Citizenship

Under the existing citizenship rule, many genuine Nepalese Madheshis failed to acquire citizenship. Table 6.8 shows that 16 percent of the sample households are yet to receive citizenship. Those who are denied citizenship complain that this has adversely affected their socio-economic conditions.

The sample population represents the Madheshi community as a whole. Therefore, the denial of citizenship to 16 percent households means the denial of this right to 16 percent of the total Madheshi population. On the basis of the population of the Madheshi community of 9.5 million, it is found that 1.5 million people are yet to acquire citizenship.

Table 6.8: Households with/without Citizenship Certificate

Categories	*Number of Households*	*Percentage*
Households with Citizenship Certificate	824	84
Households without Citizenship Certificate	158	16
Total	1000	100

Source: Field Survey. 1992.

Discrimination

According to Table 6.9, as much as 94 percent of the sample households feel discriminated by the government. Such households which feel that they are not discriminated account for only 6 percent of the sample households.

Table 6.9: Views About Discrimination

Categories	*Number of Households*	*Percentage*
Feeling Discriminated	937	94
Not feeling Discriminated	63	6
TOTAL	1000	100

Source: Field Survey, 1992

Furthermore, Table 6.10 indicates that 28 percent of the sample households feel discriminated in the fields like communication media, servicess/appointment, gover nment offices and financial institution. Besides, 25 percent of the households feel discriminated in service/ appointment followed by areas like, communication media (24 percent), government offices (21 percent), and financial institutions (2 percent).

Table 6.10 Perception About the Areas of Discrimination

Categories	*Number of Households*	*Percentage*
Communication Media	224	24
Service/Appointment	234	25
Government Offices	197	21
Financial Institutions	19	2
All of the above	263	28
Total	937	100

Source: Field Survey, 1992

Madheshis and the Army

Certain elite groups in Nepal argue that none but the Gorkhas belong to the martial race and, therefore, certain communities are not accepted in the army. However, this argument is unfounded.

It is forgotten that Harisimhadeva recruited a number of Madheshi people in the army during his rule over Kathmandu Valley in 1324 AD. At the time when Prithvi Narayan Shah attacked Jay Prakash Malla, the latter had a 12,000 strong Madheshi army who were called the Tirhutia army'.[5] The "Tirhutia army' fought very bravely against the organized forces of Prithvi Narayan Shah. Following the defeat of Jay Prakash Malla, Prithvi Narayan Shah discontinued the service of the Madheshi army. Till then, there was hardly any recruitment of Madheshi people in the Nepalese army.

It also needs to be mentioned that all the castes of people who are there in the Terai serve in the Indian army. For example, there is a separate regiment of the Rajputs and Yadavas in India. If these people could prove their worthiness in India, there is no reason why they could not do so in Nepal.

In 1992, NSP reiterated its demand for the creation of a separate 'Madheshi battalion' on the grounds that it would give the Royal Nepal Army a national character and would also strengthen national unity and national integration in Nepal. Upon this statement, The Independent, in its editorial, wrote, "This suggestion, we maintain, is a perilous one fraught with the dangers of Lebanonization of this country. A Madheshi battalion or separate battalions for Sherpas, Tharus, Thakalis, Chepangs and so on is certainly no way to boost national unity. As we see it, such a process could prove to be the beginning not of national integration but national disintegration".[6]

Expressing his reaction about the above issue in Parliament, Prime Minister G.P. Koirala stated that all the Nepalese have equal opportunity for recruitment in the Royal Nepal Army.[7] At this, Rajendra Mahato, NSP spokesman, refuted Koirala's statement and said that he (Koirala) contradicted his own address at the NC convention in Jhapa (1992) where he dared to speak the truth and demanded that "the ban on recruitment of Madheshis in the army be done away with so that they could, as others, participate in the field of national security".[8] Mahato added that the denial of the opportunity of including the Madheshi people in the army meant the denial of the rights to democracy and equality.

Regarding the charge that the army could not be created on an ethnic basis, Mahato observed that in Nepal the army is recruited on ethnic considerations and the clear example was that the Gorkha Bahadur battalion recruit Gurungs, the Kali Bahadur battalion Magars and the Pipa Headquarters Tamangs. He also added that apart from the ethnic considerations, the promotion of officers to various levels in the army was based on caste or clan considerations, which was clear from the fact that no other than a Shah, Thakuri, Rana or Chhetri had been appointed as army chief or deputy army chief. Finally, he demanded that a white paper should be issued on the ranks and number of the Madheshis in the army.[9]

The Madheshi community has been equally discriminated agaiast by the Government of India in the army service, though it is committed to protect their interests. A large number of Gurkhas are appointed in the Indian army every year. But no Madheshi is yet accepted in that army. As a result of the discrimination in the Nepalese and Indian army service, the Madheshi people are deprived of the opportunity to improve their outlook as well as economic condition.

Following the restoration of democracy in 1990, former Prime Minister Krishna Prasad Bhattarai was asked a question by the Indian journalists during his visit to India as to why the Madheshi people were neglected in the Royal Nepalese army. Replying to this question, Bhattarai wanted to know why the Government of India did not accept the Madheshi in its own army. In the Seminar on "The Terai Community and National Integration in Nepal", Narain Jha of Mahottari presented one factual story of how a Madheshi is being discriminated against in the Indian army. A gentleman from Banauli, Mahottari district, having his second name Thakur got it revised as Thakuri in the citizenship certificate and applied for service in the Indian army at Gorakhpur. After he was selected, the Indian authority found that the person recruited in the army was not Thakuri' from the Nepalese hills but Thakur' from the Terai. This was enough for the Indian authorities to terminate his service.

If the Government of India wants to have a fair image while dealing with the Nepalese citizens, it must create a separate 'Madheshi' battalion, such as Gorkha battalion of the Nepalese in its army. This will, inter alia, also provide legal status to the Terai community in asking for representation in the Royal Nepal army.

Madheshis in Politics

In most of the political parties, the leadership is in the hands of a particular ethnic group. This is one of the reasons why the Madheshis working in political parties are looked upon with distrust by the leadership.

The few Madheshis who could attain higher positions either in the political parties or in the government fail to do justice to their own community, fearing that this would add to the displeasure of certain ethnic groups. Such qualities as talent and self-respect have always been disqualifying rather than qualifying factors for the Madheshis. Persons having talent and self-respect have been discouraged and sometimes even punished.

Such Madheshis who are at the helm of affairs in the government and political parties are supposed to be yes men of certain ethnic group. Therefore, there is a grievance among the Madheshi people that only those Madheshis who could shamefully abandon their self-respect and ethnic identity could get on the top as show-pieces.

From the beginning, no influential Madheshi was tolerated by the high command in NC or such other political parties. The few Madheshi leaders who have now reached the top in politics had to quit NC when they raised their voice for due share.

History tells us that all such great Madheshi leaders, as Bhadrakali Mishra, Ram Raja Prasad Singh and even G. N. Singh had to quit NC because of discrimination against them by the NC leaders. All these leaders had been rebels during different periods of time and they had no other way but to form other political parties.

Of late, some genuine and dedicated workers of NC, like Ganesh Nepali of Mahottari and Brikhesh Chandra Lai of Dhanusha, have become the victims of NC leadership for their pro-Madheshi and pro-Hindi outlook. Both these leaders fought elections as rebel candidates and received tumultuous support from their voters.

The Madheshis and Citizenship Problem

Citizenship is a tool to participate in the governing

process of a country. The denial of citizenship affects the political, social and economic conditions of a person. It is, therefore, the fundamental right of a person to acquire citizenship.

In Nepal, the seeds of citizenship problem were sown during the regime of Prithvi Narayan Shah. The inhabitants of the Terai were not given any important assignments during his rule because they were reserved for certain ethnic groups. In the matter of assignments, first preference was given to the hill people and the second to those who settled in Nepal with their family members and who were rich, faithful and respectful. Opportunity in assignments was given to Madheshis people when individuals from the above two categories were not found. It was in rare circumstances that the Jimidari and minor government posts were assigned to them.[10]

Till the 1950s, the Madheshi people were treated like the subjects of a colony in their own country. Until 1958, it was essential for them to acquire passports before entering Kathmandu. The passport had to be obtained at Birgunj which was checked at Chisapani Garhi en route to Kathmandu.[11]

Citizenship Laws

The citizenship laws after 1950 have been made complex. In the name of controlling the influx of population from India, even certain genuine Madheshi citizens have been denied citizenship certificates. Bhadrakali Mishra told the author, "It is not a good thing that there should be an influx of people from India to Nepal. However, it is also not justified to deny the Madheshi people of their right to acquire citizenship when they have been living in this country for generations".

Present Citizenship Rule

The Constitution of the Kingdom of Nepal (1990) cites the following provisions for acquiring Nepalese citizenship:

(1) A person who is born after the commencement of this Constitution and whose father is a citizen of Nepal at the birth of the child shall be a citizen of Nepal by descent.

(2) Every child who is found within the Kingdom of Nepal and the whereabouts of whose parents are not known shall, until the father of the child is traced, be deemed to be a citizen of Nepal by descent.

(3) Whenever any territory is acquired by way of incorporation into the Kingdom of Nepal, every person having his domicile within such territory shall become a citizen of Nepal, subject to the provisions of existing laws.

(4) After the commencement of this Constitution, the acquisition of citizenship of Nepal by a foreigner may be regulated by law which may, *inter alia,* require the fulfilment of the following conditions:

(a) that he can speak and write the language of the nation of Nepal;

(b) that he is engaged in any occupation in Nepal;

(c) that he has renounced his citizenship of another country;

(d) that he has resided in Nepal for at least fifteen years."[12]

In May 1992, HMG/N announced a new "Nepal Citizenship Regulations-1992" with the objective of simplifying the procedures of acquiring citizenship. Accordingly, under clause 16 of the Nepal Citizenship Act 2020 B.S., the chairperson and vice chairperson of the Village Development Committee (VDC) were given the power to recommend the name of a person eligible for acquiring citizenship. Hitherto, such power was vested in the chairperson and vice chairperson of the District Development Committee (DDC), mayor and deputy mayor of the municipality and the gazetted employee of HMG/N. It was stated in the new regulations, "the voters list prepared for the referendum of 2037 B.S., the list prepared by the government employees deputed in all the villages to distribute citizenship certificates in 2032 B.S. and a certificate providing one's continuous service in the government and semi-government offices will serve as the basis for providing citizenship certificates under the new regulations".[13]

The new regulations also simplified the process of providing naturalized citizenship certificate. Accordingly, the foreigners wishing to obtain naturalized citizenship of Nepal were expected to apply to the chief district officer (CDO) in a specified manner with the recommendation of any one of the members, mayor and deputy mayor of the municipality; of the members, chairperson and vice-chairperson of the VDC; or of the chairperson and vice-chairperson of the DDC.

However, a writ petition was filed in the Supreme Court challenging the constitutional validity of the Nepal Citizenship Regulations 1992.[14] By the interim Order of the Court, the distribution of citizenship certificate under the Nepal Citizenship Regulations was postponed.[15]

Views of the Interviewees

The saints of the Vaishnav sect who maintain celibacy lifelong commented, "We the saints have a tradition of selecting our disciples as adopted sons. These disciples are expected to be the heirs of our property. This is what has happened right through the ages. But for certain years, our disciples are being denied this right".

Ali Mohammad Kawadi stated, "The procedures of producing necessary evidences are so complex that we do not get citizenship". Dhun Mun Harijan said, "I have settled here for the last 60 years. But I don't have any evidence to produce. So I am not getting citizenship". Dilim Bhuimali expressed, "My father died several years ago without having citizenship. When I approach the authorities concerned for my citizenship, I am told to produce the citizenship certificate of my father. Since my father did not have it, I am denied citizenship right". Likewise, Kamla Devi Yadav added, "I am being denied citizenship because my father did not have it".

Bharatendru Kumar Mallik said, "Many Madheshi people living in the Terai have been denied citizenship. On the other hand, the people of a certain community coming from foreign countries, such as India, Bhutan and Burma, get citizenship in no time".

Chet Ram Harijan reported, "The bribery at the office of the CDO creates problems in acquiring a citizenship certificate. It may not be a problem for the rich, but it is really a problem for the poor". Moreover, Chhotelal Vaishya pointed out, "I could not bribe the ward chairman for recommending my name for citizenship. Therefore, I failed to acquire it."

Birbal Prasad Kanojia maintained, "My wife is being denied citizenship as she comes from India". Dinanath Jha reported, "My wife could not get citizenship because her name was not enumerated by Nagrikta Toli (Citizenship Committee)". Similarly, Fakir Mohammad stated, "My wife is not getting citizenship though I have been sincerely trying for it. I am afraid if after my death she will be able to establish claim over our property". Furthermore, Radhe Shyam Mahato said, "My wife could not get citizenship as the concerned authorities ask for the citizenship of her father. Since her father died without having citizenship and the authorities do not give any importance to the citizenship of her mother, she has not been able to acquire this certificate."

But Manoj Kumar Jaiswal said, "We are denied citizenship because we are falsely branded as Indians". On the other hand, Satyanarayan Singh revealed, "I originate from India. But I have been teaching in Nepal for 26 years. I wish to get Nepalese citizenship. Yet I am denied of this privilege".

Causes of Citizenship Problem

Firstly, it appears from the comments that there are certain procedural complexities in acquiring citizenship. The poor and illiterate people do not know how to approach the concerned authorities for citizenship. So these people are easily exploited.

Secondly, bribery itself is a problem. Certain civil servants at CDO office are corrupt and they want to exploit the poor and illiterate people by all means. These illiterate people are forced to pay illegally. Many people give up the hope of citizenship in view of the corruption.

Thirdly, certain people are not given citizenship because their names were excluded by the citizenship committee due to certain reasons.

And fourthly, certain genuine Madheshi people are also falsely branded as Indian and on this basis they are denied their right to acquire citizenship.

Effects of Denial of Citizenship

Denial of citizenship has created problems for certain people. Firstly, they do not get service in government, corporations and private institutions. Secondly, they cannot run industry and trade. In the absence of citizenship, the industry and trade are not registered with HMG/N and consequently no loan is given by any banking and financial institution for such activities. Thirdly, denial of citizenship in one's own country means humiliation as one is treated as a foreigner. And fourthly, the denial of citizenship is the denial of the basic human rights to hold property; the reason is that nobody in Nepal is liable to purchase land in the absence of citizenship.

Methods to Promote National Integration

During the sample survey, many of the Madheshi intellectuals put forward very useful suggestions as to how the feeling of national integration could be strengthened. Such views are as follows:

Individual Views About National Integration

Akhileshwar Prasad Singh suggested, "Our present political system itself is a bottleneck in promoting national integration. Under the existing system, it is the mountains, rivers and land that are represented and not the people. This is so because representation is not held on the basis of population but on the basis of the geographical area. As such, in a district like Manang or Mustang where there is a population of only say 10,000 has one MP. But in a district, like Sarlahi in the Terai, there is a provision to have an MP on the basis of at least 100,000 population, i.e. ten times the population of Manang or Mustang". Similarly, Khadga Prasad Singh Rajbanshi added, "National integration cannot be promoted so long as election for the House of Representatives is not held on the basis of population".

Bharat Prasad Chaudhary held the view, "For promoting national integration, at least 80 to 90 percent of the revenue generated in the Terai should be spent on the development of the Terai itself. Also, the aid coming from various bilateral and multilateral institutions should be properly spent on this region".

Ganga Ram Yadav opined, "The feeling of national unity is essential. For this, it is essential that laws, rules and regulations of HMG/N are applied indiscriminately. Additionally, the registration of the associations intending to create a regional and sectarian outlook should be discouraged. In one single district Dhanusha, such organizations as, Chitragupta Seva Samiti, Gopal Seva Samiti, Marwari Seva Samiti, Rauniyar Seva Samiti, and Vaishya Seva Samiti have been registered. These organizations are based on narrow caste considerations". However, Jai Krishna Goit maintained that the organizations based on caste considerations could contribute positively in the field of social service.

Ram Krishna Jha stated, "The national integration in Nepal could be promoted if the Madheshi intellectuals are appointed in top positions, especially on the advisory board of the Royal Palace". Ramesh Kumar Jha, on the other hand, added, "The national integration in Nepal could be promoted if marriage relations are encouraged between the Madheshis and hill people".

Supat Ganesh commented, "The national integration in Nepal could be fostered if the government withdraws indirect discrimination against the Madheshi community". In this connection, Ramphal Tharu added, "Punishment should be given to those who humiliate and discriminate against the native population of the Terai".

Shiva Chandra Jha stated, "National integration could be promoted only if an effort is made by the concerned institutions to develop mutual confidence between Madheshis and the hill people". Moreover, Saktu Tharu observed, "National integration in Nepal can be promoted by providing proper education to the Madheshi community". But quite differently, Shushil Sah commented, "The Madheshi community instead of asking for reservations should be properly organized".

Collective Views About National Integration

There is a feeling among certain Madheshi intellectuals that the national integration could be promoted if "the federal system' is introduced in Nepal. Under this system, the sons of the soil would be responsible for the development of their land. This will enable the development process to become faster. Besides, this will also reduce the regional and racial feelings.

It was also stated that there should be reservation of seats for Madheshi people to the extent of 50 percent in educational institutions, civil service, army, police and other such areas.

Many interviewees stated that it is essential to be fair in listing the names of Nepalese citizens in the voter list. The names of certain ethnic group are included in the voter list where they are born; at a place where they work; and also where they migrate. On the contrary, the names of certain Madheshis are not included in the voter list even in their own home place.

Some Madheshi people also reported that the foreign organizations, like the UN agencies, foreign NGOs and the diplomatic missions working in Nepal discriminate against the Madheshi community in local appointments and other fields. It is also for this reason that the Madheshi people find it difficult to work in such organizations.

Nationalism Among the Madheshi Community

Ram Saroj Yadav, President of the District Development Committee of Dhanusha, observed that the Terai community is being discriminated against despite the fact that they are most nationalistic. Quoting B.P. Koirala, father of Nepal's democratic movement, Yadav recalled, "B.P. mentioned that it is the Terai community which is most nationalist".

Jai Krishna Goit stated that the Madheshi people have love for their soil and a genuine sense of belonging to the nation as much as any other community. Likewise, Tara Kant Jha revealed that no one could cite any example which might show that Madhesis had ever tried even a single hand action to disintegrate Nepal.

Conclusion

The ruling elites have contributed little to help the Madheshi community to get their due share in the administrative and political structure of the country. Instead, they have used all the strategies to divide and rule them. They rejoice over the bad luck of these people.[16]

It is forgotten that the hill people and Madheshis are like the two wheels of a cart and the future of the country will be bright only by maintaining a balance between the two.[17]

Of late, particularly Western education has brought in a fresh breeze of a sense of self-respect among the Madheshi intellectuals all over the country. They are now aware of their rights. Many of them have fought bravely in the democratic struggle. Some of them also attained "martyrdom'. Growth is slow but pervasive and demand for justice and equality has taken a firm footing in their activities. It is not possible to suppress their sentiments for long. This is so because ethnic autonomy is a global phenomenon and Nepal "cannot consider itself immune from such strains forever".[18]

What is, therefore, expected is to guarantee in actual practice "equal socio-economic and political participation to all ethnic groups in the nation- building endeavour. Only then, with this sort of fair ethnic policy, will all ethnic groups feel secure and satisfied and heartily join the business of nation-building".[19]

HMG/N and the political parties should give the Madheshis the right place in the decision-making process in all fields, including political, diplomatic and security sectors so that they could develop a sense of participation in the task of nation building.

The ruling elites will have to be liberal in accommodating the Madheshis in the national mainstream. Discrimination against them in the civil service, army, police, diplomatic, or political assignments will have to be removed. Persons found discriminating against any particular community should be punished.

The number of recruiting authorities from among Madheshi ethnic groups should be substantially increased. For some time, there could also be reservation of seats for the Madheshis, particularly in the army and police.

The Government of India should stop discrimination with the Madheshi community, particularly while recruiting the Nepalese in the Indian army. A separate Madheshi regiment should be created to employ the Madheshi people of Nepal in the Indian army.

A Liberal attitude should be adopted in providing citizenship to all such genuine Madheshis who have been denied this basic human rights. Apart from simplifying rules and regulations for providing citizenship, the Citizenship Committees should be formed in each two to three-year period and they should be authorized to provide citizenship certificates to the concerned people on the spot. Such Committees should visit each VDC/ TDC of the country. Sufficient care should be taken to easure that no genuine person is denied a citizenship certificate.

The existing Development Zones have been based on vertical division of geographical area covering the land area between the Nepal-China border in the north and Nepal-India border in the south. In place of this vertical division, there should be a horizontal division of the country, like the Himalayan region. Hill region and the Terai region.

An introduction federal form of constitution based on the horizontal division of the country will be useful for national integration. Autonomy, if given to the Terai region in development, will also help Nepal to make a rapid rate of growth in socio-economic fields.

There should not be two different sets of laws for the citizens in one country. Election should be held on the basis of population and not on the basis of geographical area.

One of the reasons of the Madheshi community not getting due share in the national mainstream is due to the lack of adequate consciousness. For this, education is most essential. In this context, at least two universities should be established -Janakpur University in the east and Gautam Buddha University in the west so that the Terai community could receive standard higher education in their own language.

The intellectuals could play a crucial role in creating an environment in which the people of different communities should feel that they are one. There are more points of unity than disunity among them. Religion is one of such uniting factors. A great majority of the population in the Terai and the hills are Hindus. They have equal faith in the crown. Economically, they have been made interdependent. The Terai by and large produces such products which could not be grown in the hills and vice versa. It is only through the exchange of such products that the people of the Terai and the hills could benefit. This interdependence between the two regions is unique. In fact, the Terai and hill communities, though having two different names, share the same roots as the two brothers. Democracy and prosperity of the country could be strengthened only through their mutual cooperation.

Endnotes

1. Shrestha, Nanda R., Lawlessness and Migration in Nepal, Westview Press, San Francisco,U990, pp. 166-67.
2. Himal, Sept/Oct, 1990, p. 7.
3. Shrestha, no. 1, p. 167.
4. Shaha, Rishikesh, "Guidelines from Experience" in Future of South Asia, (Ed. Chopra, Pran and el at), Macmillan India Limited, Delhi, 1986, p. 160.
5. Nepal Tarai Student Language and Culture Coordination Committee, Vichar Sangalo, Kathmandu, 1990, p. 17.
6. The Independent, September 23,1992.
7. The Independent, September 9,1992.
8. Ibid.
9. Ibid.
10. Gaige, Frederick H., Regionalism and National Unity in Nepal, Vikas publishing House Pvt. Ltd., Delhi, 1975, p. 88.

11. Ibid.
12. HMG/N, Ministry of Law, Justice and Parliamentary Affairs, The Constitution of the Kingdom of Nepal (1990), Law Books Management Board, Kathmandu, 1992, pp. 5-6.
13. The Rising Nepal, May 27,1992.
14. The Rising Nepal, June 8, 1992.
15. The Independent, June 24,1992.
16. Dahal, Dilli Ram, "Grasping the Tarai Identity", Himal, May-June, 1992, pp. 17-18.
17. Dixit, Sundar Mani, "Hamara Swapna: Madheshi Pahari Sam Bhao", (Hindi), Nav Nepal, March/April 1991, p. 16.
18. Pyakuryal, Kailash, "Ethnicity and Rural Development in Nepal: Some Ethno-Regional Concerns", paper submitted to the International Seminar on "Indo-Nepal Relations: Anthroponomical and Geo- economic Linkages" organised by the Centre for the Study of Nepal, Banaras Hindu University, March 24-26,1990, p.13.
19. Ibid.

BIBLIOGRAPHY

Books

ABC/Nepal, *Red Light Traffic: The Trade in Nepali Girls,* Kathmandu, 1993.

Ajad, R.D., *Terai Jal Rahi Hai,* (Hindi), no place, no date.

Acharya, Meena, *The Maithili Women of Sirsia,* CEDA, 1981.

Aitchison, C.U. (Compiled), *A Collection of Treaties, Engagements and Sanads Relating to India and Neighbouring Countries (Vol. II),* Superintendent Government Printing, Calcutta, 1909.

Baral, Lok Raj, *Regional Migrations Ethnicity and Security: The South Asian Case,* Sterling Publishers Private Limited, New Delhi, 1990.

Bhanu Kala Kendra, *Smarika,* (Maithili), Biratnagar, 1992.

Bista, Dor Bahadur, *Fatalism and Development: Nepal's Struggle for Modernization,* Orient Longman Limited, Hyderabad, 1992.

Bista, Dor Bahadur, *People of Nepal,* Ratna Pustak Bhandar, Kathmandu, 1987.

Blaikie, Piers and et al., *Nepal in Crisis: Growth and Stagnation at the Periphery,* Oxford University Press, Delhi, 1980.

Budamagar, Harsha Bahadur, *Kirat Bansha Ra Magarharu, (Nepali)*, Smt. Unnati Bohara, Lalitpur, 1992.

Chopra, Pran and et al. (ed.), *Future of South Asia*, Macmillan India Limited, Delhi, 1986.

Devkota, Grishma Bahadur, *Nepal Ko Rajnitik Darpan, (Nepali)*, Dhruba Bahadur Devkota, Kathmandu, 1960.

Gaige, Frederick H., *Regionalism and National Unity in Nepal*, Vikas Publishing House Pvt. Ltd., Delhi, 1975.

Gurung, Harka, *Regional Patterns of Migration in Nepal*, East West Population Institute (no place), 1983.

Jha, Makhan, *The Sacred Complex in Janakpur*, United Publishers, Allahabad, 1971.

Jha, S.K., *Indo-Nepal Relations*, Archives Books. New Delhi. 1989.

Mishra, Kiran, *Nepal Me Hindi Bhasha Avam Sahitya Ki Sthiti Ka Parigyan* (Hindi), Varanasi, 1990

Mishra, Krishna Chandra, *Nepal Ki Bhasha Samasya Samadhan Ya Takrao? Kya Chahate Hain Aap?*, (Hindi), Krishna Chandra Mishra, Kathmandu, 1990.

Moran, Kery, *Partnership for Development: forty Years of American Assistance*, USAID/Nepal, 1991.

Nepal Terai Vidyarthi Bhasha Avam Sanskriti Samanwya Samiti, *Vichar Sangalo*, (Nepali), Kathmandu, 1990.

Pant, Shastra Dutta, *Byabasthit Basti Ra Gaun Vikas*, (Nepali), South Asia Research Centre, Kathmandu, 1992.

Rajbahak, Ram Prasad, *Nepal-India Open Border: A Bond of Shared Aspirations*, Lancer Publishers Pvt. Ltd., New Delhi, 1992.

Rajbanshi, Sharmila (ed.), *Rajbanshi Bhasha Aar Ful Singh*, (Rajbanshi), Rajbanshi Bhasha Prachar Samiti, Jhapa, 1991.

Rakesh, Ram Dayal, *Folk Culture of Nepal: An Analytical Study*, Nirala Publications, New Delhi, 1990.

Rohra, Satish Kumar and Singh, Surajbhan (ed.), *Hindi Shikshan: Antarrastriya Pariprekshya,* (Hindi), Kendriya Hindi Sansthan, Agra, 1988.

Shrestha, Ishwor Govind, *The Rajbanshi: An Aboriginal Tribe,* Smt. Jamuna Shrestha, Biratnagar, 1990.

Shrestha, Nanda R., *Landlessness and Migration in Nepal,* Westview Press, San Francisco, 1990.

Singh, Kameshwara, *Mithila in India,* New Delhi, 1955.

Sharma, Ram Prakash, *Mithila Ka Itihas,* (Hindi), Kameshwar Singh Darbhanga Sanskrit Vishwavidyalaya, Darbhanga, 1979.

Shastri, Sundar Jha, *Uchastariya Jansankhya Paramarshdatri Samiti Sanga Aek Nimnastariya Byakti Ko Anurodh,* (Nepali), Janakpur Dham, 1983.

Stiller, Ludwig F., *The Rise of the House of Gorkha: A Study in the Unification of Nepal,* The Patna Jesuit Society, Patna, 1975.

Thakur, Raghunath, *Partantra Madhesh Aur Uski Sanskriti,* Raghunath Thakur, Bhalabhaleni (Morang), 1959.

Thakur, Upendra, *History of Mithila,* Mithila Institute, Darbhanga, 1956.

Thakur, Upendra, *Madhubani Painting,* Abhinav Publications, New Delhi (no date).

Vequaud, Yves, *The Art of Mithila: Ceremonial Paintings from an Ancient Kingdom,* Thames and Hudson Ltd., London, 1977.

Verma, Yugeshwar P., *Nepal: Progress and Problems,* Pratibha Verma, Jaleshwar, 1981.

Reports

Centre for Economic and Technical Studies, *Internal and International Migration and its Environmental Implications in the Nepalese Terai* (Preliminary Report), Lalitpur, 1990.

Document of the World Bank, *Nepal Relieving Poverty in a Resource Scarce Economy* (Volume I), 1990.

Document of the World Bank, *Nepal Relieving Poverty in a Resource Scarce Economy* (Volume II), 1990.

Document of the World Bank, *Nepal Policies for Improving Growth and Alleviating Poverty,* 1988.

HMG/N, Ministry of Agriculture, Department of Food and Agricultural Marketing Services, *Agricultural Statistics of Nepal 1990,* Lalitpur, 1990.

HMG/N, Ministry of Finance, *Economic Survey 1991-92,* (Nepali), Kathmandu, 1992.

HMG/N, Ministry of Law, Justice and Parliamentary Affairs, *The Constitution of the Kingdom of Nepal (1990),* Law Books Management Board, Kathmandu, 1992.

HMG/N, National Planning Commission Secretariat, Central Bureau of Statistics, *Population Census - 1991, Vol. I: Nepal,* Kathmandu, 1992.

HMG/N, National Planning Commission, Central Bureau of Statistics, *Population Census - 1991, Vol. II: Total Urban,* Kathmandu, 1992.

HMG/N, National Planning Commission, Central Bureau of Statistics, *Population Monograph of Nepal,* Kathmandu, 1987.

HMG/N, National Commission on Population, *Proceedings of the National Seminar on Population and Environment,* Kathmandu, 1989.

HMG/N, National Commission on Population, *Population and Development in Nepal,* Kathmandu, 1988.

HMG/N, National Planning Commission Secretariat, Central Bureau of Statistics, *Migration Statistics from Demographic Sample Survey 1986- 87,* Kathmandu, 1988.

HMG/N, National Planning Commission Secretariat, Central Bureau of Statistics, *Demographic Sample Survey 1986-87,* Kathmandu, 1987.

HMG/N, National Commission on Population, *Inter-Regional Migration in Nepal: Problem and Prospects,* Kathmandu, 1984.

Jan Prashashan Kendriya Shikshan Bibhag, *Jan Prashashanka Chunauti Tatha Samadhanka Upayaharu* (Nepali), Jan Prashashan Campus, Kathmandu, 1991.

National Planning Commission Secretariat, Population Division, *Nepal: Aspects of Population and Development,* Kathmandu, 1991.

National Commission on Population, *Nepalma Aantarik Tatha Antarrastriya Basai-Sarai* (Nepali), Kathmandu, 1983.

The World Bank and the United Nations Development Programme, *Nepal: Poverty and Incomes,* The World Bank, Washington D.C., 1991.

Treaty of Peace and Friendship, Kathmandu, July 31,1950.

Articles and Papers

Burghart, Richard, "The Formation of the Concept of Nation State in Nepal", *Journal of Asian Studies,* Vol. XLIV, No. 1, November 1984.

Dahal, Dilli Ram, "Grasping the Tarai Identity", *Himal,* May/June, 1992.

Dixit, Sundar Mani, "Hamara Swapna: Madheshi Pahari Sam Bhao", (Hindi), *Nav Nepal,* March/April, 1991.

Gop, Suryanath, "Upekshaon Ka Lamba Silsila Aur Terai Ka Vote Bank", *Nav Nepal,* March/April, 1991.

Jha, Hari Bansh, "Gurung Report: A Pandora's Box", *Media Nepal,* Vol 1, No. 1, 2041 Vikram Sambat.

Mishra, Hemant, "A Wild World That is No More", *Himal,* September/October, 1990.

Parmanand, "The Indian Community in Nepal and the Nepalese Community in India: Their Socio-Cultural Problems", paper submitted to an International

Seminar on Indo-Nepal Relations: Anthroponomical and Geo-Economic Linkages, Centre for the Study of Nepal, Banaras Hindu University, Varanasi, March 24-26, 1990.

Paudyal, Anant Raj, "Nepal: Ethnicity in Democracy", paper presented at the First Political Science Conference, organised by Political Science Association of Nepal, June 18-20, 1992.

Prasad, Ramashish, "The Plains People", *Himal,* September/October, 1990.

Pyakuryal, Kailash, "Ethnicity and Rural Development in Nepal: Some Ethno-Regional Concerns", paper submitted to the International Seminar on Indo-Nepal Relations: Anthroponomical and Geo-Economic Linkages, organized by the Centre for the Study of Nepal, Banaras Hindu University, March 24-26, 1990.

Shaha, Rishikesh, "Ancient and Medieval Nepal", Kailash, Vol. XV, Number 1-2, 1989.

Sharma, Prayag Raj, "How to Tend this Garden", *Himal,* May/June, 1992.

Shrestha, Bijaya Lai, "East to West, A Highway to the Future", *Himal,* September/October. 1990.

Tripathi, Aparna and Nagar, K.S., "Nepal's Ethnic Divide and India", paper presented to the International Seminar on Indo-Nepalese Relations: Anthroponomical and Geo-Economic Linkages, organised by Centre for the Study of Nepal, Banaras Hindu University, March 24-26,1990.

Journals/Papers.

Asian Survey, Vol. XXVI, No. 9. September, 1986.

Gorkhapatra, June 7, 1992.

Himal, May/June, 1992.

Himal. September/October, 1990.

Himalayan Guardian, Gangtok, July 4, 1991.

Janpukar Saptahik, February 24, 1984.

Nav Nepal. March/April, 1991.

Nepal Gazette, April 20, 1992.

The Independent, September 23, 1992.

The Independent, September 9,1992.

The Independent, June 24, 1992.

The Rising Nepal, July 8, 1992.

The Rising Nepal, June 8, 1992.

The Rising Nepal, May 27, 1992.

Sadbhavana Sandesh. October 15, 1991.

APPENDIX I

OBJECTS AND METHODOLOGY

The socio-economic conditions of the Madheshi community living in the Terai region of Nepal have been analysed in the present study on "The Terai Community and National Integration in Nepal". The basic objectives of the present study are: (1) to discuss the problems of the Madheshi community in regard to the manifestation of their language, culture and identity; (2) to review the nature of participation of the Madheshi community in the different political and administrative assignments; (3) to assess the impact of the migration of the people from the hills on the Madheshi community; (4) to analyse the economic condition of the Madheshi community; and (5) to suggest measures for improving the socio-economic conditions of the Madheshi community and also for integrating them in the national mainstream.

Considering the above objectives, the present study was based on primary as well as secondary sources for data collection. In order to collect primary data, first of all, five districts including Jhapa, Dhanusha, Parsa, Nawalparasi and Banke were selected as representative districts. Factors like language and cultural heterogeneity were considered as the basis of selecting representative districts. The Village Development Committees (VDCs) and/or Town Development Committees (TDCs) were selected from the northern, middle and southern parts of the sample districts. Each district headquarters, irrespective of whether it was in the northern, middle or southern part of a district, was included in the sampling areas.

Having identified the sampling areas, the households were selected for the interview on stratified random sampling basis. For this, the households were classified into groups, such as farmers, business persons, industrialists, service holders, wage earners and landless people. Adequate representation was given to all these groups of people in the process of sampling.

In each of the sample districts, 200 households were interviewed through a scientifically designed questionnaire. Half of these households were selected from the district headquarters. In the remaining half, 40 households were selected from the northern and 60 from the southern areas. Thus, altogether 1,000 households were interviewed in the five districts.

For supplementing the information gathered in the field, various key informants from among the Madheshi community were also consulted.

In addition to the primary data, necessary information for the study was collected from the published and unpublished research documents of the different research organizations. such as National Planning Commission (NPC), Central Bureau of Statistics (CBS), individual writers, etc.

The field survey was conducted by the enumerators during April, May and June of 1992, which were further processed and analyzed by the author. The final report of the study was completed in November 1992.

Finally, the entire report was presented at a seminar, organized at Janakpur on February 7 and 8, 1993 on "The Terai Community and National Integration in Nepal" for dissemination and comments. Each of the chapters was presented by the author at the seminar as independent papers. The discussion on the papers proved immensely useful to improve the study. Views expressed by the learned commentators and participants were duly taken into consideration while preparing the manuscript of the present book. All possible efforts were made to ensure that the study should help the process of democratization and national integration in Nepal.

APPENDIX II

REPORT OF THE SEMINAR ON THE TERAI COMMUNITY AND NATIONAL INTEGRATION IN NEPAL

The two-day National Seminar on "The Terai Community and National Integration in Nepal" was organized by the Centre for Economic and Technical Studies (CETS) in collaboration with Friedrich-Ebert-Stiftung (FES), Germany at Janakpur on February 7 and 8, 1993. The inaugural session started at 9 am on February 7, 1993. Ram Saroj Yadav, President, District Development Committee, Dhanusha, was the chairperson of the session. Megh Prasad Upadhyay, the Chief Guest, inaugurated the Seminar. Hari Bansh Jha, Executive Director of CETS, delivered the welcome address and briefed the participants on the aims and objectives of the Seminar.

Brikhesh Chandra Lai, Mayor of Janakpur Municipality, highlighted the problems being faced by the Madheshi community in Nepal. He was of the view that the privileged few would have to change their attitudes if they wanted the community to be an active partner in the task of nation building. He expressed the hope that the democratic system in Nepal could pave the way for national integration.

In his inaugural address, Megh Prasad Upadhyay stressed the need to maintain national unity. He added that it was essential to forget all our petty differences in the process of strengthening national integration in Nepal.

Lastly, in his presidential address. Ram Saroj Yadav, President of the District Development Committee, stated that the problems of the Madheshi community could no longer be overlooked. He wanted this community to remain vigilant in regard to their demand of due recognition of their culture and language as well as proportional representation in the legislature, executive and judiciary.

The first session of the seminar started formally at 11 am under the chairmanship of M. Habibullah. With the permission of the chairperson, Hari Bansh Jha presented his thought-provoking paper on "Migration and its Impact on the Terai". He expressed his observations on the subject very clearly. He also presented valuable and useful suggestions for the solution of the problems related to migration and its impact on the Terai.Commenting on the paper, Brikhesh Chandra Lal suggested that the writer could have deserved more appreciation if he had delved deeper into the problems of migration. He stated that the issue needs to be considered in the national spectrum and not as an isolated problem of the Terai region only. He added that each of the three geographical regions of Nepal, including the mountains, the hills and the Terai. have their own distinctive features. Therefore, he felt the need of specialization in these geographical areas taking into consideration the natural endowments, like local climate and soil. Such a process, according to Lal, could not merely help the development of the three geographical regions but would also reduce the flow of migration of population from the north to the south.

Another commentator on the paper, Shailendra Labh Karna, wanted clarification about the methodology of the study. Besides, he observed that the existing trend of converting state land under the forest into private land in the name of developing resettlements for squatters should be stopped and effective protection should be given to the remaining forest land in the Terai. He further added that it was high time for the concerned bodies to think seriously and evolve measures to correct the mistakes committed in the past.

Following the comments of the commentators, the floor opened for discussion. The learned participants came out with valuable ideas and suggestions. They were of the view that the government should be impartial and prompt enough to solve the problems related to migration. The session was finally concluded by M. Habibullah with his concluding remarks.

The second session started at 2:30 pm under the chairmanship of Madan Thapa, a well-known politician and lawyer of Janakpur. Hari Bansh Jha presented his paper on "The Terai and National Integration in Nepal". He threw light on the position of the Terai people in Nepal and their participation in the national programmes of the country.

After the presentation of the paper by Hari Bansh Jha, Tarakant Jha defined national integration. He was in support of the writer's feelings about the Madheshi's pitiable condition in Nepal.

The next commentator was Jay Krishna Goit. He threw light on the discriminatory attitude of the government towards the Madheshi people.

The floor discussed the condition of the Madheshi people. All the discussants were of the opinion that the responsible sections should be honest in upgrading the status of these people.

The chairperson, Thapa, thanked everyone and appreciated the useful ideas and suggestions expressed at the seminar for the national integration in Nepal.

The second-day first session of the seminar commenced at 9 am on the February 8, 1993 under the chairmanship of

Dhireshwar Jha. The paper entitled "The Language Issue in the Terai" was presented by Hari Bansh Jha.

The focus of the paper was on due recognition of Hindi in the Nepalese constitution and re-acceptance of it as the medium of instruction in the Terai.

Sundar Jha Shastri, a prominent writer and journalist, was the first commentator. He was not in favour of exhausting energy for the recognition of Hindi. The second commentator, Krishna Chandra Mishra, on the other hand, appreciated the spirit of the paper for the due recognition of Hindi in Nepal. The questions raised by participants during the floor discussion were almost in line with the views of the commentators. The paper writer Jha responded to the comments and observed that the language issue in the Terai was considered not from the point of view of the Mithila region but the Terai region as a whole and, therefore, Hindi was accorded priority over other languages spoken in the Terai. The session was concluded by Dhireshwar Jha with his useful remarks.

The second-day second session started under the chairmanship of Aasha Sinha. Hari Bansh Jha read his paper on "The Social Life in the Terai". The writer's observations on the social life of the Terai people were appreciated. He made his views clear that evil practices prevalent in the Terai society, such as, casteism, the dowry system, discrimination against women and child marriage must be uprooted by creating an awareness among common people.

Sundar Jha Shastri and Namo Narayan Jha commented on the paper. Shastri observed that the paper could have discussed distinctive features of the social life in the Terai. The floor-discussion was very informative. Various unknown facts and figures about the social life of the Terai people were brought into the picture.

The Chairperson, Sinha, expressed her happiness over the useful discussion which took place during the session.

The second-day third session of the seminar started under the chairmanship of Krishna Chandra Mishra. Hari Bansh Jha presented his paper on "The Economy of the Terai". The main concentration of the paper was on the duty-free open border trade between Nepal and India.

The first commentator on the paper was Bhogendra Jha. He made factual and logical comments on the paper. His main points were the lack of coincidence in scope and objective with the methodology of the study, contradiction in statistics and statements, improper classification of occupation, etc. He also sought justification of the duty-free open-border trade between Nepal and India. The second commentator Kameshwar Jha felt the need to make the agricultural sector more attractive.

Participants took a keen interest in expressing their views as to how to make the Terai more prosperous. Hari Bansh Jha, in response to the questions, stated that Nepal has been idea-locked rather than India-locked. The chairperson concluded the final session by making useful remarks.

The concluding session started at 6 pm under the chairmanship of Krishna Chandra Mishra. Rapporteur appraisal was presented by Shivendra Lal Karna and Surya Kant Mishra. The vote of thanks was extended to all the participants by Hari Bansh Jha. The chairperson, Krishna Chandra Mishra expressed his appreciation for the successful conclusion of the two-day seminar. He made it clear that the seminar proved an eye-opener to all.

APPENDIX III

TREATY WITH THE RAJA OF NEPAUL, 1801

Whereas it is evident as the noonday sun to enlightened understanding of exalted nobles and of powerful Chiefs and Rulers, that Almighty God has entrusted the protection and government of the universe to the authority of Princes, who make justice their principle, and that by the establishment of a friendly connection between them universal happiness and prosperity is secured, and that the more intimate the relation of amity and union the greater is the general tranquillity; in consideration of these circumstances, His Excellency the Most Noble the Governor-General, Marquis Wellesley, etc., etc., and the Maharaja have established a system of friendship between the respective Governments of the Company and the Raja of Nepaul, and have agreed to the following Articles:

ARTICLE 1

It is necessary and incumbent upon the principals and officers of the two Governments constantly to exert themselves to improve the friendship subsisting between the two States, and to be zealously and sincerely desirous of the prosperity and success of the Government and subjects of both.

ARTICLE 2

The incendiary and turbulent representations of the disaffected, who are the disturbers of our mutual friendship, shall not be attended to without investigation and proof.

ARTICLE 3

The principals and officers of both Governments will cordially consider the friends and enemies of either State to be the friends and enemies of the other; and this consideration must ever remain permanent and in force from generation to generation.

ARTICLE 4

If any one of the neighbouring powers of either State should commence any altercation or dispute, and design, without provocation, unjustly to possess himself of the territories of either country, and should entertain hostile intentions with the view of taking that country, the vakeels on the part of our respective Governments at either Court will fully report all particulars to the head of the State, who, according to the obligations of friendship subsisting between the two States, after having heard the said particulars, will give whatever answer and advice may be proper.

ARTICLE 5

Whenever any dispute of boundary and territory between the two countries may arise, such disputes shall be decided, through our respective vakeels or our officers, according to the principles of justice and right; and a landmark shall be placed upon the said boundary, and which shall constantly remain, that the officers both now and hereafter may consider it as a guide, and not make any encroachment.

ARTICLE 6

Such places as are upon the Frontiers of the dominions of the Nabob Vizier and of Nepaul, and respecting which any dispute may arise, such dispute shall be settled by the mediation of the vakeel on the part of the Company, in the presence of one from the Nepaul Government, and one from His Excellency the Vizier.

ARTICLE 7

So many elephants, on account of Muckanacinpoor, are annually sent to the Company by the Raja of Nepaul. and therefore the Governor-General with a view to promoting the satisfaction of the Raja of Nepaul, and in consideration of the improved friendly connection, and of this new Treaty, relinquishes and foregoes the tribute above-mentioned, and directs that the officers of the Company, both now and hereafter, from generation to generation, shall never, during the continuance of the engagement contracted by this Treaty (so long as the conditions of this treaty shall be in force), exact the elephants from the Raja.

ARTICLE 8

If any of the dependents or inhabitants of either country should fly and take refuge in the other, and a requisition should be made for such persons on the part of the Nepaul Government by its constituted vakeel in attendance on the Governor-General, or on the part of the Company's Government by its representative residing at Nepaul, it is in this case mutually agreed that if such persons should have fled after transgressing the laws of his Government, it is incumbent upon the principals of both Governments immediately to deliver him up to the vakeel at their respective courts, that he may be sent in perfect security to the frontier of their respective territories.

ARTICLE 9

The Maha Raja of Nepaul agrees, that a pergunnah, with all the lands attached to it, excepting privileged lands and those appropriated to religious purposes, and to jaghires, c., which are specified separately in the account of collections, shall be given up to Samee Jeo for his expenses, as a present. The conditions with respect to Samee Jeo are, that if he should remain at Benares, or at any other place within the Company's provinces, and should spontaneously farm his jaghire to the officers of Nepaul, in that event the amount of collections shall be punctually paid to him, agreeably to certain kists which may be hereafter settled; that he may appropriate the same to his necessary expenses, and that he may continue in religious abstraction, according to his agreement, which he had engraved on brass, at the time of his abdication of the Roy, and of his resigning it in my favour. Again, in the event of his establishing his residence in his jaghire, and of his realizing the collections through his own officers, it is proper that he should not keep such a one and other disaffected persons in his service, and besides one hundred men and amid servants, & c., he must not entertain any persons as soldiers, with a view to the collection of the revenue of the pergunnah; and to the protection of his person he may take two hundred soldiers of the forces of the Nepaul Government, the allowances of whom shall be paid by the Raja of Nepaul. He must be cautious, also of commencing an altercation, either by speech or writing; neither must he give protection to the rebellious and fugitives of the Nepaul country, nor must he commit plunder and devastation upon the subjects of Nepaul. In the event of such delinquency being proved to the satisfaction of the two Governments, the aid and protection of the Company shall be withdrawn from him; and in that event, also, it shall be at the option of the Raja of Nepaul whether or not he will confiscate his jaghire.

The Maha Raja also agrees, on his part, that if Samee Jeo should take up his residence within the Company's provinces, and should farm out his land to the officers of Nepaul, and that the kists should not be paid according to agreement, or that he should fix his residence on his jaghire, and any of the inhabitants of Nepaul should give him or the ryots of his pergunnah any molestation, a requisition shall be made by the Governor-General of the Company, on this subject, to the Raja. The Governor-General is security for the Raja's performance of this condition, and the Maha Raja will immediately acquit himself of the requisition of the Governor-General, agreeably to what is above written. If any profits should arise in the collection of the said pergunnah, in consequence of the activity of the officers, or any defalcation occurs from their inattention, in either case the Raja of Nepaul will be totally unconcerned.

ARTICLE 10

With the view of carrying into effect the different objects contained in this Treaty, and of promoting other verbal negotiations, the Governor-General and the Raja of Nepaul, under the impulse of their will and pleasure, depute a confidential person to each other as vakeel, that remaining in attendance upon their respective Governments, they may effect the objects above specified, and promote whatever may tend to the daily improvement of the friendship subsisting between the two States.

ARTICLE 11

It is incumbent upon the principals and officers of the two States that they should manifest the regard and respect to the vakeel of each other's Government, which is due to their rank, and is prescribed by the laws of nations; and that they should endeavour, to the utmost of their power, to advance any object which they may propose, and to promote their ease, comfort, and satisfaction, by extending protection to them, which circumstances are calculated to improve the friendship subsisting between the two Governments, and to illustrate the good name of both States throughout the universe.

ARTICLE 12

It is incumbent upon the vakeels of both States that they should hold no intercourse whatever with any of the subjects or inhabitants of the country, excepting with the officers of Government, without the permission of those officers; neither should they carry on any correspondence with any of them; and if they should receive any letter or writing from any such people, they should not answer it, without the knowledge of the head of the State, and acquainting him of the particulars, which will dispel all apprehension or doubt between us, and manifest the sincerity of our friendship.

ARTICLE 13

It is incumbent upon the principals and officers mutually to abide by the spirit of this Treaty, which is now drawn out according to their faith and religion, and deeming it in force from generation to generation that they should not deviate from it; and any person who may transgress against it will be punished by Almighty God, both in this world and in a future state.

(A true translation)

C. RUSSELL, Assistant Persian Translator.

Ratified by the Governor-General and Council, October 30, 1801, and by the Nepaul Darbar on October 28, 1802.

APPENDIX IV

TREATY OF SEGOWLEE 1815

TREATY OF PEACE between the HONOURABLE EAST INDIA COMPANY and MAHARAJAH BIKRAM SAH, Rajah of Nipal, settled between LIEUTENANT-COLONEL BRADSHAW on the part of the HONOURABLE COMPANY, in virtue of the full powers vested in him by HIS EXCELLENCY the RIGHT HONOURABLE FRANCIS, EARL OF MOIRA, KNIGHT of the MOST NOBLE ORDER of the GARTER, one of HIS MAJESTY'S MOST HONOURABLE PRIVY COUNCIL, appointed by the Court of Directors of the said Honourable Company to direct and control all the affairs in the East Indies, and by SREE GOOROO GUJRAJ MISSER and CHUNDER SEEKUR OPEDEEA on the part of MAHA RAJAH GIRMAUN JODE BIKRAM SAH BAHAUDER, SHUMSHEER JUNG, in virtue of the powers to that effect vested in them by the said Rajah of Nipal,- 2, December 1815.

Whereas war has arisen between the Honorable East India Company and the Rajah of Nipal, and whereas the parties are mutually disposed to restore the relations of peace and amity which, previously to the occurrence of the late differences, had long subsisted between the two States, the following terms of peace have been agreed upon:-

ARTICLE 1ST

There shall be perpetual peace and friendship between the Honourable East India Company and the Rajah of Nipal.

ARTICLE 2ND

The Rajah of Nipal renounces all claim to the lands which were the subject of discussion between the two States before the war; and acknowledges the right of the Honourable Company to the sovereignty of those lands.

ARTICLE 3RD

The Rajah of Nipal hereby cedes to the Honourable East India Company in perpetuity all the undermentioned territories, viz.-

First.-The whole of the low lands between the rivers Kali and Rapti.Secondly.- The whole of the low lands (with the exception of Bootwul Khass) lying between the Rapti and the Gunduck.

Thirdly. - The whole of the low lands between the Gunduck and Coosah, in which the authority of the British Government has been introduced, or is in actual course of introduction.

Fourthly. - All the low lands between the Rivers Mitchee and the Teestah. Fifthly. - All the territories within the hills eastward of the River Mitchee, including the fort and lands of Nagree and the Pass of Nagarcote, leading from Morung into the hills, together with the territory lying between that Pass and Nagree. The aforesaid territory shall be evacuated by the Gurkha troops within forty days from this date.

ARTICLE 4TH

With a view to indemnify the Chiefs and Barahdars of the State of Nipal, whose interests will suffer by the alienation of the lands ceded by the foregoing Article, the British Government agrees to settle pensions to the aggregate amount of two lakhs of rupees per annum on such Chiefs as may be selected by the Rajah of Nipal, and in the proportions which the Rajah may fix. As soon as the selection is made, Sunnuds shall be granted under the seal and signature of the Governor-General for the pensions respectively.

ARTICLE 5TH

The Rajah of Nipal renounces for himself, his heirs, and successors, all claim to or connexion with the countries lying to the west of the River Kali, and engages never to have any concern with those countries or the inhabitants thereof.

ARTICLE 6TH

The Rajah of Nipal engages never to molest or disturb the Rajah of Sikkim in the possession of his territories; but agrees, if any differences shall arise between the State of Nipal and the Rajah of Sikkim, or the subjects of either, that such differences shall be referred to the arbitration of the British Government, by whose award the Rajah of Nipal engages to abide.

ARTICLE 7TH

The Rajah of Nipal hereby engages never to take or retain in his service any British subject, nor the subject of any European and American State, without the consent of the British Government.

ARTICLE 8TH

In order to secure and improve the relations of amity and peace hereby established between the two States, it is agreed that accredited Ministers from each shall reside at the Court of the other.

ARTICLE 9TH

This treaty, consisting of nine Articles, shall be ratified by the Rajah of Nipal within fifteen days from this date, and the ratification shall be delivered to Lieut.-Colonel Bradshaw, who engages to obtain and deliver to the Raja the ratification of the Governor-General within twenty days, or sooner, if practicable.

Done at Segowlee, on the 2nd day of December 1815.

PARIS BRADSHAW, Lt.-Col.,P.A.

[Seal]

[Seal]

[Seal]

APPENDIX V

MEMORANDUM FOR THE APPROVAL AND ACCEPTANCE OF THE RAJAH OF NIPAL, PRESENTED ON DECEMBER 8, 1816

1. Adverting to the amity and confidence subsisting with the Rajah of Nipal, the British Government proposes to suppress, as much as is possible, the execution of certain Articles in the Treaty of Segowlee, which bear hard upon the Rajah, as follows:-

2. With a view to gratify the Rajah in a point which he has much at heart, the British Government is willing to restore the Terai ceded to it by the Rajah in the Treaty, to wit, the whole Terai lands lying between the Rivers Coosa and Gunduck, such as appertained to the Rajah before the late disagreement; excepting the disputed lands in the Zillahs of Tirhoot and Sarun, and excepting such portions of territory as may occur on both sides for the purpose of settling a frontier, upon investigation by the respective Commissioners; and excepting such lands as may have been given in possession to any one by the British Government upon ascertainment of his rights subsequent to the

cession of Terai to that Government. In case the Rajah is desirous of retaining the lands of such ascertained proprietors, they may be exchanged for others, and let it be clearly understood that, notwithstanding the considerable extent of the lands in the Zillah of Tirhoot, which have for a long time been a subject of dispute, the settlement made in the year 1812 of Christ, corresponding with the year 1869 of Bikramajeet, shall be taken, and everything else relinquished, that is to say, that the settlement and negotiations, such as occurred at that period, shall in the present case hold good and be established.

3. The British Government is willing likewise to restore the Terai lying between the Rivers Gunduk and Rapti, that is to say, from the River Gunduk to the western limits of the Zillah of Goruckpore, together with Bootwul and Sheeraj, such as appertained to Nipal previous to the disagreements, complete, with the exception of the disputed places in the Terai, and such quantity of ground as may be considered mutually to be requisite for the new boundary.

4. As it is impossible to establish desirable limits between the two States without survey, it will be expedient that Commissioners be appointed on both sides for the purpose of arranging in concert a well defined boundary on the basis of the preceding terms, and of establishing a straight line of frontier, with a view to the distinct separation of the respective territories of the British Government to the south and of Nipal to the north; and in case any indentations occur to destroy the even tenor of the line, the Commissioners should effect an exchange of lands so interfering on principles of clear reciprocity.

5. And should it occur that the proprietors of lands situated on the mutual frontier, as it may be

rectified, whether holding of the British Government or of the Rajah of Nipal, should be placed in the condition of subjects to both Governments, with a view to prevent continual dispute and discussion between the two Governments, the respective Commissioners should effect in mutual concurrence and co-operation the exchange of such lands, so as to render them subject to one dominion alone.

6. Whensoever the Terai should be restored, the Rajah of Nipal will cease to require the sum of two lakhs of Rupees per annum, which the British Government agreed the advance for the maintenance of certain Barahdars of his Government.

7. Moreover, the Rajah of Nipal agrees to refrain from prosecuting any inhabitants of the Terai, after its revertance to his rule, on account of having favoured the cause of the British Government during the war, and should any of those persons, excepting the cultivators of the soil, be desirous of quitting their estates, and of retiring within the Company's territories, he shall not be liable to hindrance.

8. In the event of the Rajah's approving the foregoing terms, the proposed arrangement for the survey and establishment of boundary marks shall be carried into execution, and after the determination in concert of the boundary line, Sunnuds conformable to the foregoing stipulations, drawn out and sealed by the two States, shall be delivered and accepted on both sides.

(Sd.) EDWARD GARDNER, Resident.

(Sd.) G. Wellesley, Assistant.

(A true translation.)

APPENDIX VI

SUBSTANCE OF A LETTER UNDER THE SEAL OF THE RAJA OF NIPAL, RECEIVED ON DECEMBER 11, 1816

After compliment;

I have comprehended the document under date the 8th of December 1816, or 4th of Poos 1873 Sumbut, which you transmitted relative to the restoration, with a view to my friendship and satisfaction, of the Terai between the Rivers Coosa and Rapti to the southern boundary complete, such as appertained to my estate previous to the war. It mentioned that in the event of my accepting the terms contained in that document, the southern boundary of the Terai should be established as it was held by this Government. I have accordingly agreed to the terms laid down by you, and herewith enclose an instrument of agreement, which may be satisfactory to you. Moreover, it was written in the document transmitted by you , that it should be restored, with the exception of the disputed lands and such portion of land as should, in the opinion of the Commissioners on both sides, occur for the purpose of settling a boundary; and excepting the lands which, after the cessions of the Terai to the Honorable Company, may have been transferred by it to the ascertained proprietors. My friend, all these matters rest with you, and since it was also written that a view was had to my friendship and satisfaction with respect to certain Articles of the Treaty of Segowlee, which bore hard upon me, and which could be remitted, I am well assured that you have at heart the removal of whatever may tend to my distress, and that you will act in a manner corresponding to the advantage of this State and the increase of the friendly relations subsisting between the two Governments.

Moreover I have to acknowledge the receipt of the orders under the red seal of this State, addressed to the officers of Terai between the Rivers Gunduk and Rapti, for the surrender of that Terai, and their retiring from thence, which was given to you at Thankote, according to your request, and which you have now returned for my satisfaction.

(A true translation.)

(Sd.) G. WELLESLEY, Assistant

APPENDIX VII

TREATY WITH NIPAL, - 1ST NOVEMBER 1, 1860

During the disturbances which followed the mutiny of the Native army of Bengal in 1857, the Maharaja of Nipal not only faithfully maintained the relations of peace and friendship established between the British Government and the State of Nipal by the Treaty of Segowlee, but freely placed troops at the disposal of the British authorities for the preservation of order in the Frontier Districts, and subsequently sent a force to cooperate with the British Army in the re-capture of Lucknow and the final defeat of the rebels. On the conclusion of these operations, the Viceroy and Governor-General in recognition of the eminent services rendered to the British Government by the State of Nipal, declared his intention to restore to the Maharaja the whole of the lowlands lying between the River Kali and the District of Goruckpore, which belonged to the State of Nipal in 1815, and were ceded to the British Government in that year by the aforesaid Treaty. These lands have now been identified by Commissioners appointed for the purpose by the British Government, in the presence of Commissioners deputed by the Nipal Darbar; masonry pillars have been erected to mark the future boundary of the two States, and the territory has been formally delivered over to the Nipalese Authorities. In order the more firmly to secure the State of Nipal in the perpetual possession of this territory, and to mark in a solemn way the occasion of its restoration, the following Treaty has been concluded between the two States:-

ARTICLE 1ST

All Treaties and Engagements now in force between the British Government and the Maharajah of Nipal, except in so far as they may be altered by the Treaty, are hereby confirmed.

ARTICLE 2ND

The British Government hereby bestows on the Maharajah of Nipal in full sovereignty, the whole of the lowlands between the Rivers Kali and Raptee, and the whole of the lowlands lying between the River Raptee and the District of Goruckpore, which were in the possession of the Nipal State in the year 1815, and were ceded to the British Government by Article III of the Treaty concluded at Segowlee on the 2nd of December in that year.

ARTICLE 3RD

The boundary line surveyed by the British Commissioners appointed for the purpose extending eastward from the River Kali or Sardah to the foot of the hills north of Bagowra Tal, and marked by pillars, shall henceforth be the boundary between the British Province of Oudh and the Territories of the Maharajah of Nipal.

This Treaty, signed by Lieutenant-Colonel George Ramsay, on the part of His Excellency the Right Honorable Charles John, Earl Canning, G.C.B., Viceroy and Governor-General of India, and by Maharajah Jung Bahadoor Rana, G.C.B., on the part of Maharajah Dheraj Soorinder Vikram Sah Bahadoor Shumshere Jung, shall be ratified, and the ratifications shall be exchanged at Khatmandoo within thirty days of the date of signature.

Signed and sealed at Khatmandoo, this First day of November, AD one thousand eight hundred and sixty corresponding to the third day of Kartick Budee, Sumbut Nineteen Hundred and Seventeen.

(Sd.) G. RAMSAY, Lieut.-Colonel, Resident at Nipal.

Seal

(Sd.) CANNING, Seal Viceroy and Governor-General

APPENDIX VIII

TREATY OF PEACE AND FRIENDSHIP

(Dated July 31, 1950, Kathmandu)

The Government of India and the Government of Nepal, recognizing the ancient ties which have happily existed between the two countries for centuries;

Desiring still further to strengthen and develop these ties and to perpetuate peace between the two countries;

Have resolved therefore to enter into a Treaty of Peace and Friendship with each other and have, for this purpose, appointed as their plenipotentiaries the following persons, namely,

The Government of India:

His Excellency Shri Chandreshwar Prasad Narain Singh, Ambassador of India in Nepal.

The Government of Nepal:

Maharaja Mohun Shamsher Jang Bahadur Rana, Prime Minister and Supreme Commander-in-Chief of Nepal,

Who, having examined each other's credentials and found them good and in due form have agreed as follows:

Article I

There shall be everlasting peace and friendship between the Government of India and the Government of Nepal.

The two Governments agree mutually to acknowledge and respect the complete sovereignty, territorial integrity and independence of each other.

Article II

The two Governments hereby undertake to inform each other of any serious friction of misunderstanding with any neighbouring state likely to cause any breach in the friendly relations subsisting between the two Governments.

Article III

In order to establish and maintain the relations referred to in Article I the two Governments agree to continue diplomatic relations with each other by means of representatives with such staff as is necessary for the due performance of their functions.

The representatives and such of their staff as may be agreed upon shall enjoy such diplomatic privileges and immunities as are customarily granted by international law on a reciprocal basis:

Provided that in no case shall these be less than those granted to persons of a similar status of any other State having diplomatic relations with either Government.

Article IV

The two Governments agree to appoint Consuls-General, Consuls, Vice- Consuls and other consular agents, who shall reside in towns, ports and other places in each other's territory as may be agreed to.

Consuls-General, Consuls, Vice-Consuls and other consular agents shall be provided with exequaturs of other valid authorization of their appointment. Such exequatur or authorization is liable to be withdrawn by the country which issued it, if considered necessary. The reasons for the withdrawal shall be indicated wherever possible.

The persons mentioned above shall enjoy on a reciprocal basis all the rights, privileges, exemptions and immunities that are accorded to persons of corresponding status of any other State.

Article V

The Government of Nepal shall be free to import, from or through the territory of India, arms, ammunition or warlike material and equipment necessary for the security of Nepal. The procedure for giving effect to this arrangement shall be worked out by the two Governments acting in consultation.

Article VI

Each Government undertakes, in token of the neighbourly friendship between India and Nepal, to give to the nationals of the other, in its territory, national treatment with regard to participation in industrial and economic development of such territory and to the grant of concessions and contracts relating to such development.

Article VII

The Government of India and Nepal agree to grant, on a reciprocal basis, to the nationals of one country in the territories of the other the same privileges in the matter of residence, ownership of property, participation in trade and commerce, movement and other privileges of a similar nature.

Article VIII

So far as matters dealt with herein are concerned, this Treaty cancels all previous treaties, agreements and arrangements entered into on behalf of India between the British Government and the Government of Nepal.

Article IX

This Treaty shall come into force from the date of signature by the Governments.

Article X

This Treaty shall remain in force until it is terminated by either party by giving one year's notice.

APPENDIX IX

LETTER EXCHANGED WITH THE TREATY

(Dated the 31st July 1950, Kathmandu)

EXCELLENCY,

In the course of our discussion of the Treaties of Peace and Friendship and of Trade and Commerce which have been happily concluded between the Government of India and the Government of Nepal, we agreed that certain matters of details be regulated by an exchange of letters. In pursuance of this understanding, it is hereby agreed between the two Governments:

(1) Neither Government shall tolerate any threat to the security of the other by a foreign aggressor. To deal with any such threat, the two Governments shall consult with each other and devise effective counter-measures.

(2) Any arms, ammunition or warlike material and equipment necessary for the security of Nepal that the Government of Nepal may import through the territory of India shall be so imported with the assistance and agreement of the Government of India. The Government of India will take steps for the smooth and expeditious transport of such arms and ammunition through India.

(3) In regard to Article 6 of the Treaty of Peace and Friendship which provides for national treatment, the Government of India recognize that it may be necessary for some time to come to afford the Nepalese nationals in Nepal protection from unrestricted competition. The nature and extent to this protection will be determined as and when required by mutual agreement between the two Governments.

(4) If the Government of Nepal should decide to seek foreign assistance in regard to the development of the natural resources of, or of any industrial project in Nepal, the Government of Nepal shall give first preference to the Government or the nationals of India, as the case may be, provided that the terms offered by the Government of India or Indian nationals, as the case may be, are not less favourable to Nepal than the terms offered by any other Foreign Government or by other foreign nationals.Nothing in the foregoing provision shall apply to assistance that the Government of Nepal may seek from the United Nations Organization or any of its specialized agencies.

(5) Both Governments agree not to employ any foreigners whose activity may be prejudicial to the security of the other. Either Government may make representations to the other in this behalf, as and when occasion requires.

Please accept Excellency, the assurances of my highest consideration.

(Sd.) MOHUN SHAMSHER JANG BAHADUR RANA
Maharaja, Prime Minister and Supreme Commander-in-Chief of Nepal

To: His Excellency

Shri Chandreshwar Prasad Narain Singh. Ambassador Extraordinary and Plenipotentiary of India at the Court of Nepal, Indian Embassy, Kathmandu.

INDEX

I

J

K

L

M

N

■■■